Jonathan Ha

Canary

Methuen Drama

Published by Methuen Drama 2010

1 3 5 7 9 10 8 6 4 2

Methuen Drama
A & C Black Publishers Limited
36 Soho Square
London W1D 3QY

www.methuendrama.com

ISBN 978 1 408 13104 6

A CIP catalogue record for this book is available
from the British Library

Typeset by Mark Heslington Limited, Scarborough, North Yorkshire
Printed and bound in Great Britain by CPI Cox & Wyman, Reading, Berkshire

Liverpool Everyman and Playhouse, English Touring Theatre and Hampstead Theatre present

CANARY
A New Play by Jonathan Harvey
Directed by Hettie Macdonald

First performed on Friday 23 April 2010
at the Liverpool Playhouse

ETT
ENGLISH
TOURING
THEATRE

Hampstead Theatre

About the Everyman and Playhouse

Liverpool Everyman and Playhouse together make up a single engine for creative excellence, artistic adventure and audience involvement. In recent years the theatres have been on a remarkable journey, described as "a theatrical renaissance on Merseyside" (Observer).

The theatres have repeatedly collaborated with partners beyond Liverpool and the UK, taking work to new audiences and putting Liverpool theatres firmly on the national cultural map. Recent productions include a West End transfer of Harold Pinter's *The Caretaker*, directed by Christopher Morahan and starring Jonathan Pryce, currently playing at the Trafalgar Studios, a co-production of *The Hypochondriac* with English Touring Theatre, and *King Lear* starring Pete Postlethwaite with Headlong and the Young Vic.

Current collaborations include *Ghost Stories* by Andy Nyman and Jeremy Dyson, now breaking box office records with co-producers Lyric Hammersmith following a Liverpool world première. Future collaborations include a co-production of *The Ragged Trousered Philanthropists* in a new adaptation by Howard Brenton with Chichester Festival Theatre in June 2010.

But there is more to these theatres than simply the work on our stages. We have a busy Literary Department, working to nurture the next generation of Liverpool Playwrights. A wide-ranging Community Department takes our work to all corners of the city and surrounding areas, and works in partnership with schools, colleges, youth and community groups to open up the theatre to all.

To find out more about our work, both on and off stage, call 0151 709 4776 or visit **www.everymanplayhouse.com**

Two great theatres. One creative heart.

Liverpool Everyman and Playhouse is a registered charity No.1081229

King Lear Amanda Hale & Pete Postlethwaite
© Stephen Vaughan

The Caretaker Jonathan Pryce
© Helen Warner

Ghost Stories Andy Nyman
© Helen Warner

Supported by
ARTS COUNCIL ENGLAND

Thanks to Liverpool City Council for its financial support

Liverpool City Council

Knowsley Council

ETT
ENGLISH TOURING THEATRE

surprise • delight • enrich • engage

Under the direction of Rachel Tackley, ETT presents potent, vivid and vital productions of new and classic plays to audiences far and wide.
A powerhouse of touring theatre, ETT works with a rich and varied mix of the country's leading directors, actors and artists to stage thrilling and ambitious theatre that is vigorous, popular and, above all, entertaining.

In 2009... ETT presented 407 performances... to 147,000 people

In 2010:

Rum & Coca Cola
A bittersweet tale by celebrated Trinidadian dramatist,
Mustapha Matura,
directed by **Don Warrington MBE**.
ETT, Talawa and West Yorkshire Playhouse.
UK tour – autumn 2010

Love Song
Soul legend, **Omar,**
in an uplifting tale of love,
directed by **Che Walker**.
Touring - May to August 2010
UK tour - autumn 2010

Marine Parade
A play with songs by **Simon Stephens**;
music by **Mark Eitzel**.
***ETT** and **animalink** at the
Brighton Festival, May 2010*

The Three Musketeers
& the Princess of Spain
A family show by **Chris Hannan**.
*At the Traverse Theatre, the
Belgrade Theatre, Coventry and on
tour - October - December 2010*

ett.org.uk

Supported by
ARTS COUNCIL ENGLAND

●● **BRITISH**
●● **COUNCIL**

Hampstead Theatre

Hampstead Theatre is one of the UK's leading new writing companies - a company that has just celebrated its fiftieth year of operation.

Throughout its long history the theatre has existed to support a thriving local, national and international playwriting culture. We commission plays in order to enrich and enliven this culture. We support, develop and produce the work of new writers, emerging writers, established writers, mid-career writers and senior writers and have a proud tradition for creating the conditions for their plays and careers to develop.

The list of playwrights who had their early work produced at Hampstead Theatre and who are now filling theatres all over the country and beyond include Mike Leigh, Michael Frayn, Brian Friel, Terry Johnson, Hanif Kureishi, Simon Block, Abi Morgan, Rona Munro, Tamsin Oglesby, Harold Pinter, Shelagh Stephenson, debbie tucker green, Crispin Whittell, Roy Williams and Dennis Kelly.

The Creative Learning programme is also an integral part of Hampstead Theatre's work. We aim to celebrate all aspects of the creative process in ways which support learning and widen access to the theatre's programme. Inspiring creativity and developing emerging talent, at its best our work has the power to change lives.

In recent years we have been proud to establish a strong tradition of collaborating with some of the country's leading repertory and touring theatre companies, including producing *3 Sisters on Hope Street* with Liverpool Everyman and Playhouse in 2008. We are delighted to be working with Liverpool once again on *Canary*, and collaborating with English Touring Theatre.

Hampstead Theatre, Eton Avenue, Swiss Cottage, London NW3 3EU
www.hampsteadtheatre.com
Registered Charity number: 218506

Supported by

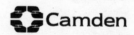

Credits

Cast (in alphabetical order)

Ben Allen	Mickey
Sean Gallagher	Older Russell
Philip McGinley	Younger Tom
Jodie McNee	Melanie
Ryan Sampson	Younger Russell
Kevin Trainor	Billy
Philip Voss	Older Tom
Paula Wilcox	Ellie

Other parts played by members of the company
The play is set mostly in Liverpool and London, between 1962 and the present day

Company

Writer	**Jonathan Harvey**
Director	**Hettie Macdonald**
Designer	**Liz Ascroft**
Lighting Designer	**Colin Grenfell**
Sound Designer	**Jason Barnes**
Assistant Director	**Dan Ayling**
Costume Supervisor	**Jacquie Davies**
Casting Directors	**Gemma Hancock CDG &**
	Sam Stevenson CDG
Production Manager (Liverpool)	**Sean Pritchard**
Production Manager (ETT)	**Felix Davies**
Company Manager	**Paul Sawtell**
Stage Manager	**Sarah Lewis**
Deputy Stage Manager	**James Theobold**
Assistant Stage Manager	**Jake Bartle**
Lighting and Sound Operators	**Mark Goodall & Jenny Tallon-Cahill**
Stage Crew	**Jason McQuaide & Mike Grey**
Wardrobe Mistress	**Brenna McKenzie**
Wardrobe Maintenance	**Tracey Thompson**
Set built by	**Q Division**
Scenic Print Graphics	**Servicegraphics**
Video Design	**Joe Stathers-Tracey**
Front Cover Image	**Eureka Design Consultants**

The company wishes to thank:

Andrew Davies at Food Chain
Richard Foord
Brian Paddick
Peter Tatchell
Mike Brown at LIPA

Graham Norton
Katie Bryant, Company Manager of
Les Miserables at the Queens Theatre

Cast

Ben Allen
Mickey

Ben trained at East 15 Acting School.

Theatre credits include:
All's Well That Ends Well and *The History Boys* (National Theatre); *Noises Off* (Ambassador Theatre Group) and *Louisville in London* (Riverside Studios).

Television credits include:
Bonekickers.

Short film include:
Better Than Joe.

Sean Gallagher
Older Russell

Theatre credits include:
The Black Album (National Theatre); *Cleansed* (Oxford Stage Company / Arcola Theatre); *Mayhem* (Manchester Royal Exchange Studio); *The Quare Fellow* (Oxford Stage Company / Tricycle Theatre); *Out In The Open* (Hampstead Theatre / Birmingham Rep); *Outside On The Street* (Gate Theatre); *Brothers of The Brush* (Liverpool Everyman); *Don Juan* (National Theatre Studio); *Half Past One* and *The Fairy Tale* (Greenwich Studio); *Oktoberfest* (Lyric Studio); *Butley* and *Cut It Out* (Dukes, Richmond) and *Volpone* (Cambridge Theatre Company).

Television credits include:
Holby City, Heartbeat, Rock Rivals, Coronation Street, New Street Law, Doctor Who, Class of 76, Murder Prevention, Island at War, Ella and The Mothers, Clocking Off, Linda Green, Micawber, Border Café, Extremely Dangerous, Under The Sun, Touching Evil, Holding On, The Tenant of Wildfell Hall, The Change, Silent Witness, Christmas, House of Windsor, History File, Casualty, Murder Most Horrid, Peak Practise, The Bill, Eastenders, Boon, The Guilty and *Downtown Lagos*.

Film credits include:
Making a Killing, Offending Angels, Elephant Juice, His'n'Hers, La Passione, Jock of The Bushveld and *Wedlock*.

Radio credits include:
The Golden Notebook and *24 Weeks*.

Cast

Philip McGinley
Younger Tom

Theatre credits include:
More Light (Arcola Theatre);
The Changeling (Cheek By Jowl);
Great Expectations (RSC) and *Kes*
(Royal Exchange Theatre).

Television credits include:
*The Gemma Factor, Coronation Street,
The Bill, Casualty, Cold Blood, Heartbeat,
Blue Murder, Falling, Battlefield Britain,
Hawking, The Deputy* and *Dalziel and
Pascoe.*

Jodie McNee
Melanie

Theatre credits include:
Knives In Hens and *Jenufa* (Arcola Theatre);
When We Are Married (West Yorkshire
Playhouse / Liverpool Playhouse); *A Taste of
Honey* (Royal Exchange Theatre); *King Lear*
(The Globe); *Cymbeline, The Changeling*
and *Gilgamesh Workshop* (Cheek By Jowl);
Mother Courage (English Touring Theatre)
and *The Burial at Thebes* (Nottingham
Playhouse).

Television credits include:
Poirot, Criminal Justice 2, Liverpool Nativity
and *Shane II.*

Film credits include:
A Picture of Me.

Cast

Ryan Sampson
Younger Russell

Theatre credits include:
Brighton Beach Memoirs (Watford Palace Theatre); *Dido - Queen of Carthage, DNA* and *The Miracle* (National Theatre); *Monsieur Ibrahim and The Flowers of The Quran* (Bush Theatre); *A Brief History of Helen Troy* (Soho Theatre / UK Tour); *Over Gardens Out* (Southwark Playhouse) and *Richard III* and *Edward II* (Sheffield Crucible).

Television credits include:
After You've Gone (Three Series), *Doctor Who, The Things I Haven't Told You, Holby City, Heartbeat, In Denial of Murder* and *Wire In the Blood.*

Kevin Trainor
Billy

Theatre credits include:
Six Degrees of Separation (Old Vic); *Bent* (Trafalgar Studios); *Twelfth Night, Solstice, The Comedy of Errors* and *Eric LaRue* (RSC); *Lost Monsters* (Liverpool Everyman); *Gladiator Games* (Stratford East Theatre Royal); *2000 Feet Away* (Bush Theatre) and *Love Labour's Lost* (Rose, Kingston).

Television credits include:
John Adams, Tripping Over, The Catherine Tate Show, The Commander and *Titanic: Birth of a Legend.*

Film credits include:
Hellboy and *Make It New John.*

Radio credits include:
The Hiring Fair.

Cast

Philip Voss
Older Tom

Philip Voss is an Associate Actor of
the RSC and his many productions
with them include *Coriolanus, The
White Devil, The Alchemist, Artists and
Admirers, Wallenstein, A Midsummer
Night's Dream* and *Troilus and Cressida.*

Other recent theatre credits include:
*The Wandering Jew, Countrymania,
The Strangeness of Others, Peer Gynt,
Piano, Abingdon Square, Ivanov, Love's
Labour's Lost, The Royal Hunt of the
Sun* and *The Mikado* (The Royal National
Theatre); *The Seagull, Three Sisters and
Marriage* (Shared Experience); *As You
Like It, The Royal Family* and *Much Ado
About Nothing* (The Peter Hall Company);
The Giant (Hampstead Theatre); *3 Sisters
on Hope Street* (Liverpool Everyman
and Hampstead Theatre); *The Circle*
(Chichester Festival Theatre) and
Apologia (The Bush Theatre).

Television credits include:
*Second Sight, Bad Company, The
Dwelling Place, A Village Affair, A Royal
Scandal, Where the Heart is, Let Them
Eat Cake, Fish, North Square, Trial and
Retribution, Dinotopia* and *Brides in
the Bath.*

Film credits include:
*Indian Summer, Mountains of the Moon,
Clockwise, Lady Jane, Octopussy, The
Secret Rapture, Stranded, Four Weddings
and a Funeral* and *Frankenstein and the
Monster from Hell.*

Philip's many radio broadcasts include:
Lord of the Rings and *Embers.*

Paula Wilcox
Ellie

Theatre credits include:
Dreams Of Violence (Soho Theatre);
La Cage Aux Folles (Playhouse Theatre);
*Whatever Happened to the Cotton
Dress Girl* (New End Theatre); *General
Review of the Sex Situation* (Jermyn Street
Theatre); *The (Female) Odd Couple*
(West End); *The Memory of Water*
(No1 Tour); *Blithe Spirit* (Palace Theatre,
Watford) *Same Time, Another Year*
(No1 Tour); *The Clowness* (Gate
Theatre); *Candida* (New End Theatre);
Mr Wonderful (Derby Playhouse); *Listen
to the Wind* (King's Head Theatre); *The
Comedy of Errors* (Regent's Park Open
Air Theatre); *The Queen and I* (Vaudeville
Theatre); *The Comedy of Errors*
(Nottingham Playhouse); *Raving Beauties*
(Liverpool Playhouse); *Serious Money*
(LA Theatre Works) and *Shirley Valentine*
(Duke of York's Theatre).

Television credits include:
*Moving On, Touch of Frost, Emmerdale,
Blue Murder, Green, Green, Grass,
Doctors, The Smoking Room, Murder
in Suburbia, Down to Earth, Viva Las
Blackpool, Merseybeat, Holby City,
Footballers Wives, The Queen's Nose,
Peak Practice, The Stalker's Apprentice,
Life After Birth, Smokescreen, Blue
Heaven, Casualty, Fiddlers Three, Boon,
Mrs Capper's Birthday, Remember the
Lambeth Walk?, The Bright Side, Peter
Cook and Friends, Miss Jones and Son,
Man About the House* and *The Lovers.*

Film credits include:
Outlaw directed by Nick Love and *Scoop*
directed by Woody Allen.

Company

Jonathan Harvey
Writer

Theatre credits include:
Jack And the Beanstalk (Barbican Theatre);
Closer To Heaven (Really Useful Group);
Out In The Open (Hampstead Theatre /
Birmingham Rep); *Hushabye Mountain*
(English Touring Theatre / Hampstead
Theatre); *Guiding Star* (Liverpool Everyman /
National Theatre); *Swan Song* (Pleasance
Theatre / Hampstead Theatre); *Rupert
Street Lonely Hearts Club* - Manchester
Evening News Award For Best New
Play (English Touring Theatre / Donmar
Warehouse / Criterion Theatre); *Boom
Bang-A-Bang* (Bush Theatre); *Babies* -
Evening Standard Award For Most
Promising Playwright (Royal Court Theatre);
Beautiful Thing - John Whiting Award
Winner (Bush Theatre / Donmar
Warehouse); *Wildfire* and *Mohair* - Rank
Xerox Young Writers Award Winner
(Royal Court Upstairs) and *The Cherry
Blossom Tree* - National Girobank Young
Playwright Of The Year Award (Liverpool
Playhouse).

Television credits include:
Beautiful People (Two Series - winner:
Best comedy BANFF TV Festival),
*Britannia High, Octavia, Lilies, The Catherine
Tate Show, Cinderella: The Big Brother
Panto, Best Friends, Twisted Tales, Von
Trapped!, Coronation Street; Margo
Leadbetter: Beyond the Box, At Home
With The Braithwaites, Birthday Girl,
Big Smoke, Gimme Gimme Gimme*
(Three Series), *Murder Most Horrid,
West End Girls* and *Rev.*

Film: *Beautiful Thing* (London Lesbian And
Gay Film Festival Best Film Award / GLAAD
Awards, New York For Outstanding Film).

Radio: *Take That Lennon And Sid.*

Hettie Macdonald
Director

Theatre credits include:
*On Insomnia and Midnight, The Thickness
of Skin, Talking In Tongues, A Jamaican
Airman Forsees His Death, Maydays
Dialogue, William* and *The Plague Year*
(Royal Court, London); *MAD* and
Beautiful Thing (Bush Theatre); *Top Girls*
(Citizens Theatre, Glasgow); *She Stoops
To Conquer* (New Kent Opera); *Sanctuary*
(National Theatre); *The Storm* (Almeida
Theatre); *The Yiddish Trojan Women*
(Soho Theatre Company); *Beautiful Thing*
(Duke Of Yorks / Donmar Warehouse);
All My Sons (Oxford Stage Company);
*The Slicing Edge, Road, The Nose,
Once In A While The Odd Thing Happens,
A View from the Bridge, Deathtrap,
Margaret Catchpole, A Dolls House,
Absent Friends, Who's Afraid Of Virginia
Woolf, The Scarlet Pimpernel* and
The Three Sisters (As Associate Director
of the Wolsey Theatre, Ipswich);
The Madman of the Balconies (Gate
Theatre); *The Party's Over* (Nottingham
Playhouse); *Brighton Beach Memoirs*
(Salisbury Playhouse); *Waterland* (Eastern
Angles/Shaw Theatre); *A Pricksong for
the New Leviathan* (Old Red Lion); *Leave
Taking* (WPT / Lyric Hammersmith);
A Midsummer Night's Dream (Chester
Gateway); *Beware of Pity* (National
Theatre Studio); *Heartgame* (Soho Poly);
The Normal Heart (Albery Theatre) and
Shamrocks and Crocodiles (Liverpool
Playhouse).

Opera credits include:
Hey Persephone! (Almeida Theatre /
Aldeburgh Festival).

Television credits include:
*Wallander, Marple - Murder is Easy,
The Fixer, White Girl, Doctor Who - Blink,
Banglatown Banquet, Poirot - Mystery
of the Blue Train, In A Land of Plenty,
William and Mary, Servants, Hearts and
Bones, Where The Heart Is* and *Casualty.*

Film credits include:
Beautiful Thing.

Company

Liz Ascroft
Designer

Liz graduated with BA Hons from Wimbledon School of Art. She has been awarded the Arts Council Trainee Design Bursary, the UNESCO award for Promotion of the Visual Arts (Prague Quadrennial), and TMA Best Designer.

Theatre credits include:
Lucia Di Lammermoor (Scottish Opera); *Grapes of Wrath* (RADA); *On Golden Pond, Golden Leaf Strutt, Sad Arthurs Trip* and *Agnes of God* (Belgrade Theatre Coventry); *Trojan Women, Tis Pity She's a Whore, As You Like It* and *The Nativity* (Liverpool Everyman); *Alice's Adventures in Wonderland, A Midsummer Night's Dream, The Importance of Being Earnest, The Three Musketeers, The Snow Queen, Death and the Maiden, Robin Hood* and *Beauty and the Beast* (Dukes Playhouse, Lancaster); *Merrily We Roll Along* (Watermill Theatre); *Blithe Spirit, The Three Sisters, Children's Hour, Strawgirl, The Adoption Papers, Roots, Mary Barton, Hedda Gabler, As You Like It, Fast Food, So Special, The Seagull, The Rise and Fall of Little Voice* and *On the Shore of the Wide World*, which transferred to The Cottesloe Theatre, (Royal Exchange Theatre, Manchester); *Katherine Howard* (Chichester Festival Theatre); *Cavalcaders* (Tricycle Theatre); *Seven Up, Vincent River, Apocalyptica, Give me Your Answer Do, Yellowman, Anna in the Tropics, Losing Louis* and *Rubenstein's Kiss* (Hampstead Theatre); *Peggy For You* (Comedy Theatre, London and Tour); *Two Gentlemen of Verona* (RSC - Swan Theatre and National Tour) and *Honour* (Wyndham's Theatre, London).

For The Gate Theatre Dublin:
All My Sons, Uncle Vanya, Pygmalion, Dublin Carol and *See You Next Tuesday* (The Duke Of York's, London); *The Bear* and *Afterplay* (The Spoleto Festival, South Carolina and The Gielgud Theatre London); *Faith Healer, Yalta Game* and *Afterplay* (The Sydney Festival) and

Harold Pinter's *One for the Road* (St Martin's Theatre London), which transferred with *A Kind of Alaska* to The Lincoln Centre, New York for The Pinter Festival.

Short film includes:
Shadow Man.

Liz is currently working on *Lucia Di Lammermoor* for Houston Grand Opera, Texas.

Colin Grenfell
Lighting Designer

Recent theatre includes:
The Caretaker (Liverpool Everyman, West End); *Unprotected* (Liverpool Everyman); *Mine* (Shared Experience); *I am Yusuf and this is my brother* (Young Vic); *The Elephant Man* and *Equus* (Dundee Rep); *When the Rain Stops Falling* (Almeida Theatre); *365, The Bacchae* and *Black Watch* (National Theatre of Scotland); *The Thief of Baghdad* (Royal Opera House); *Single Spies* (Theatre Royal Bath); *Alex* (Arts Theatre); *Theatre of Blood, Spirit, The Hanging Man, Lifegame, Coma, Animo* and *70 Hill Lane* (Improbable); *Kes* and *Separate Tables* (Manchester Royal Exchange); *Touched* (Salisbury Playhouse); *Enjoy* (Watford Palace Theatre) and *Casanova* and *Playing the Victim* (Told by an Idiot).

Opera credits include: extensive work for Opera Holland Park; *Fidelio* (Opera Touring Company Dublin) and *La boheme* (English Touring Opera).

Company

Jason Barnes
Sound Designer

Jason has been involved with theatre sound for over 15 years, designing sound for productions throughout the UK. Jason was also Head of Sound and resident Sound Designer for Bristol Old Vic from 1999 - 2007.

West End Sound Designs include:
Mrs Warren's Profession (Comedy Theatre and UK tour); *Private Lives* (Vaudeville Theatre); *Enjoy* (Gielgud Theatre and UK tour) and *We're Going on a Bearhunt* (Duchess Theatre and UK tour).

Other theatre:
Juliet and Her Romeo (Bristol Old Vic); *Hansel and Gretel* (Bristol Old Vic and Kneehigh Theatre UK tour); *Quadrophenia* (Plymouth Theatre Royal and UK tour); *Once Upon a Time at the Adelphi, Noises Off* and *Dr Faustus* (Liverpool Playhouse); *Home* (Bristol Old Vic Studio); *Low Pay? Don't Pay!, What the Butler Saw* and *Alphabetical Order* (Salisbury Playhouse); *A Small Family Business* (Watford Palace Theatre) and *Unprotected* (Liverpool Everyman).

As resident Sound Designer at Bristol Old Vic, shows include:
The Three Musketeers, The Importance of Being Earnest, The Barber of Seville and *Tamburlaine* (Bristol and Barbican); *The Odyssey* (Bristol, Liverpool and West Yorkshire Playhouse); *Private Peaceful* (Bristol and tour) and *Up the Feeder Down the 'Mouth and Back Again, A Streetcar Named Desire* and *Blues Brother Soul Sisters*.

Other Sound:
Sound Engineer, *Rapunzel* for Kneehigh Theatre (UK tour and adaptation for the off-Broadway venue, New Victory Theatre NYC).

Dan Ayling
Assistant Director

Dan is a graduate of the MFA in Theatre Directing at Birkbeck and was Runner Up for the JMK Young Director's Award 2007.

He is co-Artistic Director of Cheekish Productions.

Directing credits for Cheekish include:
Shoot/Get Treasure/Repeat and *Eschara* (UK tour / Union Theatre); *Christie in Love* (Lion & Unicorn); *Contrarotulus* (Best Overall Production, Daffodil Awards 2009) and *Shoot/Get Treasure/Repeat* and *Eschara* (Brighton Festival).

Freelance directing credits include:
Bridge of Dreams and *Cricket Remixed* (Almeida); *Can't Stand Up For Falling Down* (Arcola); *The Kiss* (Hampstead Theatre) and rehearsed readings at Soho and Riverside Studios.

As an assistant director, Dan has worked at Shakespeare's Globe, Lyric Hammersmith, Sheffield Theatres, Perth Rep, Hampstead Theatre, on tour, in the West End and in New York. He has worked for directors including Lucy Bailey, Katie Mitchell and Cathie Boyd, and Daniel Kramer, Phillip Prowse and Will Tuckett.

Company

Jacquie Davies
Costume Supervisor

Theatre credits include:
Dick Whittington, The Caretaker, Lost Monsters, Billy Wonderful, Mother Goose, Endgame, Eric's, Intemperance, The Way Home, The Morris and Port Authority (Liverpool Everyman); *Ghost Stories, The Hypochondriac, The Price, Our Country's Good, Tartuffe* and *Once Upon a Time at the Adelphi* (Liverpool Playhouse); *Vurt, Wise Guys, Unsuitable Girls* and *Perfect* (Contact Theatre, Manchester); *Oleanna* and *Memory* (Clwyd Theatr Cymru); *Love on the Dole* (The Lowry, Manchester); *Never the Sinner* (Library Theatre, Manchester) and *Shockheaded Peter* (West End).

Opera credits include work at:
Scottish Opera, Buxton Opera Festival, Music Theatre Wales and Opera Holland Park.

Television and film credits include:
Queer As Folk, The Parole Officer, I Love The 1970s and 1980s, Brookside and *Hollyoaks.*

Design credits include:
Kes, Saturday, Sunday, Monday, Oh What a Lovely War, Into the Woods, The Rover, Titus Andronicus, Pericles, Spring Awakening, Twelfth Night, Macbeth, The Red Balloon, The Weirdstone of Brisingamen, Perfect, The Cherry Orchard, Machinal and *Trelawny of the Wells. The Taming of the Shrew* (Wilton's Music Hall); *Dr Faustus* and *The Taming of the Shrew* (Bristol Old Vic); *A Passage to India* (Shared Experience); *Macbeth* (Albery) and extensive work at Soho, Chichester and the Royal Shakespeare Company.

Television and film credits include:
The Kingdom, Notes on a Scandal, George Orwell - A Life in Pictures (Emmy Award Winner), *The Bill* and *The Falklands Play.*

Radio credits include:
The Conflict is Over, The Leopard, Felix Holt the Radical, The Pickwick Papers, Tender is the Night and *The Bride's Chamber.*

Gemma Hancock & Sam Stevenson CDG
Casting Directors

Theatre credits include:
Where There's a Will, Love's Labour's Lost, The Portrait of a Lady, A Doll's House, The Vortex, Uncle Vanya, Pygmalion, Little Nell, Amy's View, Habeas Corpus, Measure for Measure, You Never Can Tell, Waiting for Godot, Much Ado About Nothing, The Dresser, As You Like It and *Man & Superman* (directed by Peter Hall); *Ring Round the Moon, Waiting for Godot* and *Breakfast at Tiffany's* (directed by Sean Mathias); *In the Club, Honour, What the Butler Saw* and *Abigail's Party* (directed by David Grindley); *Private Lives, Blithe Spirit, Don Juan, Tejas Verdes, Emperor Jones* and *The Chairs* (directed by Thea Sharrock); *The Deep Blue Sea* (directed by Edward Hall); *The Odyssey* (directed by David Farr); *Miss Julie* and *Everything is Illuminated* (directed by Rachel O'Riordan); *The Lieutenant of Inishmore* (directed by Wilson Milam); *Alice's Adventures in Wonderland, Beasts and Beauties* and *Watership Down* (directed by Melly Still) and *Ghosts* (directed by Anna Mackmin).

Television and film include:
Money, Emma, Consuming Passion, Silent Witness, The Inspector Lynley Mysteries, Mr Loveday's Little Outing, Rough Crossings, The Romantics, Peter Ackroyd's London, The Bill, My Life as a Popat, Holby City, EastEnders, Babel (UK Casting) and *The New World* (Casting Associate).

Canary

For Richard and Kumari

Introduction

'Women and gay people are the litmus test of whether a society is democratic and respecting human rights. We are the canaries in the mine.' Peter Tatchell.

Five or six years ago I sat having lunch in a posh Japanese restaurant in Soho, pitching television series ideas to the Heads of Drama at ITV with the other members of my production company at the time, my partner Richard and our Head of Development Kumari Salgado. I can't remember the ideas we were throwing at them and it was hard to see their reactions as – it being a very posh Japanese restaurant – it was so dimly lit you couldn't even see the menu in front of your face. We were attempting to offer them what they claimed they wanted: fun, female-skewed, high-concept comedy drama ideas about Lottery winners, single mums finding their mojo and cross-dressing gorillas taking over the world. (Okay, I made that one up. Mind you, I'd probably watch it.) There was an awkward pause and one of the Drama bods said 'Yes Jonathan, but what is it you *really* want to write about? Forget what our agenda is. If we said to you you had carte blanche to write any television series you could . . . what would it be?'

Well. That was a no brainer. I'd long been interested in writing something that contextualised where the gay community is today. A story that would attempt to encapsulate what it has been like to be gay in this country over the last, say, fifty years. I just didn't think a major TV channel would be interested in it. But as we discussed it a waitress came and put a candle on our table (was there a power cut I wondered? no, it was just a pretentious eaterie) and suddenly I could see that the Drama Chiefs' faces had illuminated too. They thought there was something in this. I went away to start work.

Eventually they passed on the idea in a rather abrupt volte face as they'd just been offered a follow up to *The Naked Civil Servant* and John Hurt was attached. As so often happens in my career I was told they couldn't make it because they were already doing their gay drama for that year. Woe betide there'd be two of the damn things! So we discussed the idea with Channel 4 who offered similar praise but explained that they were making Kevin Elyot's *Clapham Junction*, which had *loads* of gays in it!

By then Kumari and I had done a lot of research, we were experts in British Gay History. I just wanted someone to let me write about it. Maybe I should have stuck with the cross-dressing gorillas taking over the world. But in these days of ever decreasing television budgets and the homogenising of drama, I guess it would have ended up being a low budget thing about smartly dressed gorillas taking over Manchester. And I'm just not sure it would have worked.

A few years later I went to talk to Gemma Bodinetz at Liverpool Playhouse to discuss writing a play for her. In a brightly lit office Gemma – who directed my plays *Guiding Star* and *Closer To Heaven* – asked if I had anything burning I wanted to write about. I thought of my telly idea. Would it be possible to take the stories I had read during my research and make a piece of theatre from them? It felt like a mammoth task, and so I shied away from it, chosing instead to write a simple three act play about a group of friends in Liverpool and seeing them in the eighties, the nineties and the present day. Gemma organised a workshop of it. On the second day I realised I'd made a big mistake. I'd not delved deep enough. I'd not told the stories I'd wanted to tell, the stories I remembered from my research. Stories about aversion therapy, AIDS, combination therapy, survivor guilt, bug chasers, the Gay Liberation Front. I told Gemma I was throwing that play away and starting again.

Canary was an ambitious piece to write. I knew I wanted to write about an older gay couple, tracing their relationship from the sixties to the present day. I also knew I wanted to write about a younger couple, best mates, tracing them from the eighties to the present day. What would their experiences say about the gay community? Is there a gay community any more? There was so much I wanted to say, felt I *had* to say, but how could I shape the material to make a coherent story that was bigger than just a Gay History Piece? How would the men be linked? How would their paths cross? As I pieced together their journeys I hit upon a bold idea that would link the four men. I'm not going to give it away here in case you've not seen or read the play yet, but I was quite proud of it, I have to say!

Sue Townsend once said she felt playwrights wrote best when they were angry about something. I'm not sure what I'm angry about, possibly never having had the chance to write about those cross-dressing gorillas, but I do know I am passionate about the gay experience. I am passionate that the lesbians and gay men who went before me and fought for the relative liberties I have today should be remembered and thanked. I am passionate that the younger generation should not become complacent.

As I was finishing the play I worried that perhaps contextualising where we are today wasn't a strong enough idea for a piece of theatre. Was I just reminding all us 'lucky bitches' it wasn't always so? Have we got it easy? Does it really matter? And then I heard about a gay man being killed on Trafalgar Square, and then a young gay man beaten to within an inch of his life leaving a gay bar in Liverpool. And it made me want to carry on.

Not all writing is perfect. But I can forgive rough edges if it's written from the heart. Nothing irritates me more than stuff that's 'written from the wrist'. (What was it Gore Vidal said? 'That's not writing it's typing!') *Canary* is the piece of theatre I am most proud of writing. I hope you enjoy it. I wrote it from the heart.

I would just like to thank my partner Richard Foord for being the best encyclopaedia on gay history I have ever known – my own personal Hall-Carpenter archive! I'd like to say a big thank you to Kumari Salgado for all her hours of painstaking research into the themes of the play. And finally I'd like to thank my director, Hettie Macdonald, who at every stage of the development process has asked the right questions and pushed me. I hope I've done her proud.

Jonathan Harvey
2010

Characters

Tom, *from Liverpool. The Police Commander for a prominent London borough.*

Billy, *his lover, from Northern Ireland.*

Russell, *openly gay ex-West End musical leading man turned primetime TV host.*

Mickey, *Russell's best friend growing up.*

Ellie, *Tom's long suffering wife.*

Melanie, *their neurotic daughter.*

Tom's Father, *also a policeman.*

Mary Whitehouse, *guardian of the nation's morals.*

Robin, *Mickey's older lover.*

Boy, *Ellie's fantasy son.*

Dr Tony McKinnon, *a specialist in aversion therapy from Lancashire.*

Frank, *a striking miner.*

Sue, *his wife.*

Young Ellie

Toby, *a young dancer on Russell's TV show.*

Judge

Policeman 1

Policeman 2

Mrs Ford, *a head waitress.*

Margaret Thatcher, *the Prime Minister.*

Norman Fowler, *Secretary of State for Health.*

Vicar, *a right-wing homophobe.*

Nurse

At the Festival of Light:

Various members of the GLF disguised as:

Mouse Woman	**Onlooker**
Porn Woman	**Nuns**
Porn Woman 2	**Security Guards**
Toilet Woman	**Klu Klux Klan Members**

Setting

The play is set mostly in London and Liverpool, from 1960 to the present day.

Prologue – Lecture Hall, 1970

Lights up on **Mary Whitehouse**, *standing at a lectern, addressing a gathering.*

Mary   Ladies and gentlemen there is a scourge in our society and it is wholly unchristian. Right beneath our very noses permissiveness is occurring at every opportunity. Why, even yesterday, walking my neighbour's shitsu, I came across a page from a magazine. At first I thought is was an avant garde advertisement for sausages. I thought, 'She's peckish'. But no. It was a page ripped from a pornographic magazine, ladies and gentlemen. Anybody could have come across it. And it was lying in the gutter on Michaelmas Drive.

(Beat.)

If we can save questions for later I'll be more than happy to answer them thank you, Dylis.

(Beat.)

What I wish to share with you today is my vision. Colin?

The back wall illuminates with a map of Britain. And a symbol saying Festival of Light.

Mary   Lovely Colin Green there. What he does with his Mongoloid daughter brings tears to the eyes, it really does.

(She clears her throat.)

Ladies and gentlemen. In twelve months from now. In the year of our Lord 1971. I propose we stage the country's very first Festival of Light. The Festival will make a stand against moral darkness. In particular, pornography, abortion and, of course, homosexuality. I'm sorry if those words offend anyone in the audience but we have to face these repugnancies head on.

We need to know what we're fighting. And we need to be unafraid. And so I will ask you all to join in with me. Say the

word. Don't be frightened of the devil. Say the word.
Homosexual. Homosexual. Louder! Homosexual!!

(*And so on. Eventually*)

I think it might be time for a prayer.

The lights fade on **Mary** *and come up on Act One.*

Act One

Scene One – Mickey's house, Billericay, 1979

Sixteen year old **Mickey** *doing some interpretive dance in his Mum's front garden in time to* Because The Night *by Patti Smith, dressed in her wedding dress, for all the world to see. Presently sixteen year old* **Russell** *cycles past on his bike. He stops at* **Mickey***'s gate and watches him.* **Mickey** *stops, stares him out, and then starts to spin round and round. It's a dizzying sight which unnerves* **Russell***.* **Mickey's Mum** *calls from indoors.*

Mickey's Mum   Michael? Are you wearing my wedding dress again?!!

Mickey *stops spinning.*

Mickey   No!

Mickey's Mum   Wait til your father gets home!!

Russell *is tickled by this.* **Mickey** *smirks at him, then starts spinning again.* **Russell** *gets back on his bike and cycles off.*

Blackout.

Scene Two – Tom's house, Islington, 2010

The music stops abruptly. Forty-six year old **Russell***'s bike is propped up against the sofa.* **Tom***, sixty-five, hands out some drinks. Behind them, tall sash windows look onto other town houses and a black night sky. A drinks cabinet and a buttoned up leather sofa. Tom's wife* **Ellie** *sits on the settee.*

Russell   I don't want a drink.

Tom   Then why are you shaking?

Ellie   Can someone *please* tell me what is going on?

Russell   I don't take any pleasure in this.

Tom   This young man has come with . . .

Russell   It's a while since I've been called that.

Tom   Rumours, lies.

Ellie   About what? What?

Tom   I'd rather wait 'til Melanie gets here.

Ellie   Well why are we still entertaining him, if he's . . .

Russell   Oh, you're being entertaining are you? I had no idea.

Tom   Can you not be so rude to my wife?

Ellie   Can't we just kick him out on the street?

Russell   Not many family photos in evidence here are there?

Tom   She's here.

Ellie   There's no show without Punch.

Tom (*To* **Russell**.)   You keep your mouth shut.

There is something of a commotion outside. **Tom** *swiftly exits. The front door goes, revealing the flash of a hundred paparazzi bulbs, then he returns with his daughter* **Melanie**. *She is about thirty and has a slightly manic air. During the scene,* **Tom** *takes out a navy blue handkerchief and turns it over and over in his hands, nervously.*

Melanie   What's going on? They nearly tore me to shreds coming in. I couldn't see a thing, all those lights flashing, hands grabbing. They've ripped my dress. Look at my dress. Mother have you got a needle and thread? People like that. Beasts. I don't think they'll be happy 'til they've drawn blood. (*Sees* **Russell** *and shrieks.*) Oh my God it's you!!

Tom   Sit down Melanie.

Melanie   What's he doing here? What's going on? Do you have any cotton Mother?

Tom   Melanie please.

Melanie   Lilac if possible. I can't believe you've got a celebrity in your . . .

Russell   I've . . . known your parents for quite some time.

Ellie   We're hardly bosom pals.

Tom (*To* **Russell**.)   Will you please wipe that smirk off your face!

Melanie   How long will they be there? I'm not going out there again. I can't. (*Dialling a number on her mobile.*) I'll have to stay.

Tom   They might be bugging your phone.

Melanie   What?!! Can they do that? What have you done? (*On phone.*) Simon, something dreadful's happened, I don't know what but basically I'm gonna have to stay here the night.

Ellie   How serious is this?

Melanie (*pause*)   Well give her some tinned peaches for fuck's sake! (*Hangs up.*) Arabella's at a very troublesome age.

Tom   I've . . . obviously . . . got something to tell you.

Melanie   Is the guest room made up? Or is it taken? (*She motions towards* **Russell**.)

Ellie   He's not staying.

Russell   Look, they're awaiting a response from your Father. To a story.

Melanie *gets a sewing kit out of a drawer, slips her skirt off and sits. She starts mending her skirt.*

Melanie   A story? How exciting! Will it be like primary school? Shall we all have a glass of milk and sit cross legged on the floor? I might pick a scab as I listen, just for effect.

Tom   I'm so sorry Ellie. I don't have the foggiest idea how this has come about.

Ellie (*To* **Melanie**.)   I can't believe you just did that.

Melanie *looks up and realises she was addressing her.*

Melanie   Why? *He*'s hardly going to be bothered. (*Indicates* **Russell**, *then addresses him.*) That's so typical of her.

Russell   Tomorrow *The News Of The World* are running a story about your Father having . . . a kind of affair.

Melanie   Ooh! There's life in the old dog yet.

Russell   A love affair, I think.

Melanie   Love? Nice to know you're capable of it.

Tom   You think?

Russell   I'd say the cameras out there were a bit of a giveaway.

Ellie (*To* **Russell**.)   And what business is it of yours?

Melanie   With who? With who? My God!

Russell *sees* **Ellie** *looking at him.*

Russell   Don't look at me!

Tom   Ellie!

Ellie (*To* **Russell**.)   I wouldn't put anything past you.

Melanie (*To* **Ellie**.)   You don't still use that ghastly fabric conditioner do you? With the flowers? Last time I stayed I got the most awful rash. Oh and now I've pricked my thumb.

Tom   You know Melanie, sometimes silence is golden.

Russell   What, like you never owning up to the truth?

Tom   Funny how the cameras only turned up after you'd arrived. What did you do? Tip them off?

Russell   I don't need this.

Melanie   Who is it? Oh not that awful secretary of yours. Glasses. Three different hairstyles on the one head.

Tom   Don't be stupid Melanie.

Russell   My arrival was altruistic.

Tom   If you say so.

Melanie   Mother why is Mr Saturday Night in our living room?

Russell   You know I don't just do presenting stuff. I'm actually an actor, first and foremost.

Ellie   I wish someone would tell me. I was just reading *Wolf Hall* when . . .

Melanie   Oh, isn't it vile. All those words.

Tom   When have I even had time for an affair?

Russell   It's certainly not his secretary. It's a bloke. A guy.

Ellie   Yes we know what bloke means.

Beat.

Melanie   I'm sorry?

Ellie   Right, well there's a simple solution to this. Just deny it. Make a statement. Phone someone. Tell them all it's nincompoop.

Melanie   They can't print lies like that, you should sue.

Russell   And what if it's not lies?

Ellie   You're a lot fatter than you are on the telly.

Melanie   Is this some sort of joke? Dad? Well?

Tom *says nothing.*

Melanie   Dad, there are fifty blokes outside with zoom lenses, answer the bloody question!!

Ellie   This isn't about you, Melanie. Much as you'd like it to be.

Suddenly **Melanie** *bursts out crying.* **Russell** *looks at her, bewildered.*

Melanie   I live on my nerves. I'm by nature a very nervous person.

Russell   They have evidence of you meeting with a prisoner.

Tom   I run a police force. I see prisoners every day of my life, I can't believe this is happening.

Melanie (*To* **Russell**.)   Why are you here?

Russell   Someone told me. I got a tip off. I came round here to give him the heads up.

Melanie   But why you?

Russell   Your Father and I have history!

Ellie   Will you have to resign?

Melanie   He's the Chief of Police, Mother, of course he'll have to resign!

Ellie   Not if he denies it. This family will not be held to ransom by the gutter press.

Tom   The whole thing's ridiculous.

Russell   It's not just the affair, it's everything.

Ellie (*Unsure*.)   Everything?

Russell   Yes, everything. In case you've forgotten, you last saw me at . . .

Ellie   I know full well where I last saw you. You might think twenty years can erase the memory, but, unfortunately. No.

Russell   Twenty four. Almost a quarter of a century.

Ellie   You might think I'm stupid to have put up with him all these years but I can assure you I'm very much not.

Russell   I do not think you're stupid.

Ellie   Can you get out of my house please? Now? You always bring bad luck.

Melanie   What happened twenty-four . . .

Ellie   What are you? The devil? Whenever I see you. Chaos. Pain. Get out!

Tom   He can't go now. He goes now and it'll be proof positive I'm a queer. He'll be all over the press.

Melanie   You can't say queer now, Dad, unless you are one.

Ellie   Melanie. Take this man.

Russell   My name is Russell.

Ellie   It's a nice evening. Go on the patio, it's not overlooked. Get drunk together. Have that bottle of Chateau Lafite.

Melanie   The one you were saving for a rainy day?

Ellie   The heavens just opened. I want to speak to your Father alone.

Melanie   Why did you ask me round here?

Tom   Oh and you'd rather read this in the papers tomorrow? When you're feeding your brat of a daughter?

Melanie (*To* **Ellie**.)   If it's true . . .

Ellie   They can print what they like. We'll refute it.

Melanie   You have to leave him Mother. I always hated Mary Archer.

And she exits. **Russell** *goes to follow then falters.*

Ellie   Don't you dare say anything to her about . . .

Russell   About what?

Ellie   She lives on her nerves. She's by nature a very nervous person.

Russell   And what's to stop me walking out of that front door now?

Tom   The past.

Russell   You should be ashamed of yourself.

Russell *goes.* **Ellie** *looks to* **Tom**.

Ellie   Should you? I'm not a mind reader.

Tom   I need to think.

Ellie   We'll just deny it. Everything. Brave face. United front.

Tom (*Snapping*.)   An it's that easy, is it!

Ellie   I'm going upstairs.

Tom   Ellie, no, I'm sorry.

Ellie   I just want to run. And keep on running.

And she hurries out. Left alone **Tom** *eventually stands up. He wanders round the room, hands in pockets, deep in thought. Eventually he clears his throat. And starts to sing.*

Tom   If you're fond of sand dunes and salty air
Quaint little villages here and there
You're bound to fall in love with Old Cape Cod.

The lights fade, and rise on:

Scene Three – Billy's bedsit, Liverpool, 1962

The lights come up on seventeen year old **Tom**, *lying in bed with his mate* **Billy** *in the middle of the afternoon. They're both smoking.* **Tom** *is singing to* **Billy**. **Billy** *is from Ireland.*

Tom   If you like the taste of a lobster stew
Served by a window with an ocean view
You're sure to fall in love with old Cape Cod.

Billy   Tom? Tom, can I ask you something?

Tom   D'you like that? Heard it on the radio.

Billy   Are you courting that girl from church? Plays the organ?

Tom   I've only got to hear a song once and I remember it.

Billy   Is it serious?

Tom   Ellie's a nice girl.

Billy   With an arse the size of a roundabout.

Tom   Billy. This. Messing around. It's . . . it's kids' stuff.

Billy   I don't feel like a kid. Not when I'm with you.

Tom   You are a kid, saying stuff like that.

Billy   Be honest. You'd rather have a dollop of this than what you get up to with Ellie. Or are you saving stuff like that 'til you're married?

Tom   I wish it was before.

Billy   Before?

Tom   You don't ask many questions. You just get on with it. And then afterwards. You're like this. You could set your watch by it.

Billy   There was a thing in the paper. How To Spot A Homo. D'you wanna see?

Tom   Billy don't.

Billy *gets a hidden copy of* The Mirror *out from under the mattress.*

Billy   The easy way to pick a pervert is they all wear corduroy pants and have girls' hair apparently.

Tom   You won't find any cord in my wardrobe.

Billy   Apart from that pleated skirt.

Tom   Billy, if you're worried. About this carrying on. Getting in the way of marriage. The future. It won't. One day we'll put a stop to it.

Billy   Is that what you want?

Tom   You read too much into things. Reading papers. Thinking too much.

Billy   Suede shoes. Sports jacket. Smoking a pipe apparently. Oh and walking at ninety five degrees. They're the dead giveaways according to *The Mirror*.

Tom   I don't know what walking at ninety five degrees means.

Billy   Bit like you really.

Tom *grabs him and they play fight for a while.* **Billy** *wins. He has him pinned to the bed.*

Billy   I wish we could stay like this forever.

Tom   I'd get rigor mortis eventually.

Billy   The smell of you. Everything about you.

Tom   Billy.

Billy   I don't care.

Tom   You should.

Billy   Head in the clouds, me.

Tom   And I start my shift at three.

Billy *lets him go.* **Tom** *gets up to get dressed. He puts his jacket on. It's part of a police uniform.*

Billy   If you wanna come the picture house, you can sit in the projectionist's booth with me. On Tuesdays and Thursdays Old Harry lets me do it all on me own. Come in your uniform and I might even polish your buttons for you.

And they kiss again. Suddenly the door bursts open and three **Policemen** *run in.*

Policeman 1   Get off the bed the pair of you, come on!

Policeman 2   And get your hands off him you, you dirty invert!

Policeman 1   Evil bastards, now! Come on! (*To other copper.*) Get the sheets, that's evidence. Yous two are coming down the station with me. Dirty sodomites, d'you hear me?

Billy   Hey! Get off him!

Tom   It's not how it looks! I swear to God.

Policeman 1   (*mimicking him*) I swear to God. Pissing yourself are you lad? Shitting a brick are you?

Tom   I swear to God. You don't know what happened.

Policeman 1   I wasn't born yesterday you know.

Tom   You don't though.

Billy   Shut up Tommy.

Policeman 2   Yeah, save your breath for the station! And get some clothes on, the pair of you! Come on! Step on it! Jesus!

Blackout.

Scene Four – Tom's back garden, Islington, 2010

Melanie *and* **Russell** *are drinking posh wine in the back garden.* **Melanie** *is pacing about. There are two patio chairs and a table.*

Russell   I so don't want to be here.

Melanie   Snap! The thing with my family is they never really speak. They just shut down when anything big's happening. Acres of silence. Poor GCSE results. Silence. My first miscarriage. Condemning looks. When the cat died they didn't tell me for two weeks. Well it felt like two weeks. Could you?

She hands him her glass. She gets a little bag of coke out and a key and starts shovelling some on.

Melanie   Little livener?

Russell   D'you think that's wise?

Melanie   You front a reality show that puts people in the chorus lines of West End Musicals. Don't talk to me about wise.

Russell   Fair point. (*He snorts it.*)

Melanie   And then there was the big one. Oh God, someone should write a book about my life.

Russell   I'll get my Dictaphone out.

Melanie *snorts some coke.*

Melanie   Mother was the local organist. Always had more time for that blessed choir than she did for me. And I'm tone deaf, to her eternal shame. She took me to watch them practicing one night. Couldn't get a babysitter. She's there, beating time with a knitting needle. I've explored this a million times with my therapist. When the door at the back opens and this guy comes in. He took her to one side and said something to her. She nodded. He left. Then she carried on with the practice.

Russell   That's good stuff.

Melanie   In the car on the way home I said 'What did that man say?' She said 'Your brother's dead. He came off his moped on the outskirts of Tring.' (*She lets this settle.*) She carried on as if nothing had happened. Gammon for supper. Pineapple rings. I had a tantrum because she'd run out of spaghetti hoops.

Russell   Where was your Dad?

Melanie   Away on a course. He went on a lot of courses. Needless to say I'm scared witless of anything on two wheels.

Suddenly there is a beep of a horn. A scream of breaks. And then the sound of a car colliding with a motorbike. **Ellie** *rushes through, putting on a fur coat.*

Melanie   My God what was that?

Ellie   Don't go out front, you know it'll only upset you.

Melanie   Is anyone hurt?

Ellie   I'm going out to see.

Melanie   Mother! Since when did you have a fur coat?

Ellie (*taps forehead*)   Up here I'm Bette Davies. Do you have a cigarette?

Melanie   I've only got one left

Ellie   I'll mime that bit.

Melanie   Bette Davies?

Ellie   Tonight, everyone comes out. Wish me luck.

And she heads off. **Melanie** *turns to* **Russell**.

Melanie   I should do less drugs.

Russell   It's my favourite word. More. Come on then!

And she gets some more coke out and they sniff a bit more.

Melanie   Russell? Can I call you Russell?

Russell   It's my name.

Melanie   Do you think the natural human condition is to feel depressed?

Russell   Erm, that's a bit deep.

Melanie   Sorry. I have a tendency to be inappropriate.

Russell   Whenever I feel isolated, alone. I think of this friend I used to have. You'd've loved him. Sit down.

Melanie   Are you going to tell me a story?

They sit.

Russell   I was crap. And he was so amazing. We ran away to London together and he was the brightest star in Heaven.

Blackout.

Scene Five – Heaven nightclub, 1981

Lights, dry ice, action! We find eighteen year old **Mickey** *dancing on a podium by the dance floor at Heaven nightclub. He is lost in the music. He takes a big snort of poppers and sings along to the song at the top of his voice. It's Boys Town Gang and* 'Remember Me'.

Mickey (*sings*)   Remember me as a sunny day
That you once had along the way
Didn't I inspire you a little higher
Remember me as a funny clown
That made you laugh when you were down

As he sings, eighteen year old **Russell** *struggles on carrying two holdalls and a guitar case, looking most put out.*

Russell   Can we go please?

Mickey (*sings*)   Didn't I boy, didn't I boy

Russell   Mickey there's no women in this club.

Mickey (*sings*)   Remember me as a big balloon

Russell   Mickey? Have you brought me to a gay club?

Mickey (*sings*)   At a carnival that ended too soon

Russell   I've got our bags.

Mickey (*sings*)   Remember me as a breath of spring

Russell   Please? Can we go?

Mickey (*sings*)   Remember me as a good thing.

Russell   My spot cover's wearing off, I'll look like a Belesha Beacon in a minute.

Mickey   All right, all right, keep your hair on tiger.

Russell   Where we gonna go? We've got nowhere to go.

Mickey   Isn't that part of the adventure?

Russell   But we've run away to London and we've got nowhere to sleep. I should never have listened to you.

Getting off the train. 'Ooh let's go dancing', he says. 'I just wanna dance' he says. Yeah well look at us now. We shoulda gone and found a B and B there and then. I should've followed my instincts. You've spent all our savings on booze.

Mickey   Oh shut up Russell, I've sorted us a bed for the night.

Russell   Who with?

Mickey   This bloke I met in the toilets. He said we could go back to his. Come on, it'll be a laugh.

Russell   I can't believe the situations you put me in sometimes.

Mickey   Don't worry, straight boy, you won't have to do nothing. Leave that to me. You'll like him, he's posh. He's an opera singer.

Russell (*more interested*)   Oh right.

Mickey   So he'll be hitting top C tonight, d'you know what I'm saying?

Russell   And he doesn't mind me coming back an'all?

Mickey   I always look after you don't I?

Russell   Maybe he could give me some advice.

Mickey   Yeah. Lighten up, you're getting on everyone's tits.

Russell   About my acting.

Mickey   Just don't bore him with it, all right? You do my head in, talking about it all the time. Right he's coming over. Smile.

Robin *comes in. A bit older than them, dressed like a clone. Big moustache.*

Mickey   All right Robin? How's it going? This is my mate Russell I was telling you about. Russ, this is Robin.

Russell   Hi.

Robin   Ooh it's my lucky night.

Mickey   Oh no, he won't be putting out. Bit of a fridge our Russell int you mush?

Russell   I'm actually straight, so . . .

Mickey *and* **Robin** *laugh at this.* **Russell** *is stung.*

Robin   And you've just moved to London?

Russell   Yeah that's right.

Robin   Where from?

Russell / **Mickey**   Essex.

Robin   Oh.

Mickey   Billericay. D'you know it?

Robin   I haven't had that pleasure.

Russell   Mickey says you're an opera singer.

Robin   I'm a violinist actually. At the ENO.

Mickey   Oh I musta misheard when I had your knob in my ear.

Russell   That's a rather impressive moustache you have Robin.

Robin   Thank you. Shall we go?

Mickey   Yeah, all these poppers are giving me a headache.

Russell *picks up all the bags.* **Robin** *gives him a hand.*

Robin   I'm surprised you didn't bring the kitchen sink. Come on. We can carry on the party at home.

Russell   Where is it you live?

Robin   Archway.

Russell   Ooh that sounds nice. Doesn't it sound nice Mickey?

Mickey   Have a snort of them and shut your mouth.

He hands **Russell** *the poppers as they head out.*

Blackout.

Scene Six – a roundabout in Tring, 2010

Ellie *walks across a deserted street where the dead body of a young man lies. The music stops abruptly.*

Ellie   Is there nobody here to help this boy?

(*She takes out a mobile phone.*)

I can't get a signal.

(*She makes to return home.*)

Where's my house gone? My street? Where am I?

Suddenly the body sits up. He gives her a start. There is blood all over his face.

Ellie   Is it you?

Boy   They came for me.

Ellie   You look different.

Boy   What time is it?

Ellie   You sound different.

Boy   Is it eight o'clock?

Ellie   How many times have I told you?

Boy   I'm meeting this lad at eight. Outside the station. This is a new top.

Ellie   You should always wear your crash helmet.

Boy   Will you help me get ready?

Ellie   I'm not sure this is real time.

Boy   All these bits. What are these bits?

Ellie   Where's your bike?

Boy   Is it my brain?

Ellie   Are we in Tring?

Boy   Are you a nurse?

Ellie   Are all the roads yellow in Tring?

Boy   I need to go to the station.

Ellie   Where's your crash helmet?

She wanders to look for his crash helmet.

Boy (*like his dying words*)   You're not my Mum.

Ellie   I can't find it.

When she turns, he has gone.

Ellie   Where did you go?

She looks around.

Ellie   Which way do I go now?

She heads off.

Blackout.

Scene Seven – Robin's house, 1982

Russell *is in bed on a sofa bed, reading.* **Robin** *comes downstairs and watches him.*

Robin   Where's Mickey? I thought he was out with you.

Russell   Yeah he was. I lost him.

Robin   D'you know what time it is?

Russell   About two?

Robin   What you reading?

Russell   *The Cherry Orchard.* We're doing it at drama school. Well one of the teachers has written a musical version of it. Cherries!

Robin *sits on the sofa bed and suddenly weeps.*

Robin   He treats me like shit Russell.

Russell   I know.

Robin   Stop covering for him. I know you're covering for him. Is he off with some fancy piece? I bet he's with some bit of . . . rough trade from . . . Turnham Green or . . . He'll tell me about it when he gets in. Oh he's very generous like that. It has a certain boyish appeal. I'm just a bit sick of it, truth be told.

Russell   Robin. It's really kind of you to let us stay. I know we ain't given you any money and that, but . . .

Robin   I don't need money. You think I need money? I had a rather marvellous aunt. Left me a fortune. I've got a very big heart you see Russell. Give give give.

Russell   And we really appreciate it.

Robin   See, why can't he be like that? Why can't he be like you? Manners of a Duchess. Did I tell you I met the Queen Mum once?

Russell   You did.

Robin   Fisted one of her footmen below stairs at Clarence House. Exquisite cornices. Am I ugly?

Russell   No.

Robin   I am.

Russell   You're really handsome.

Robin   Would you think me terribly forward if I kissed you Russell?

Russell   I'm straight.

Robin   You're studying musical theatre. You wear legwarmers through choice. I've seen you checking out my crotch. I'll ask you again.

Russell   I'm a bit scared.

Robin   I'm not that intimidating am I?

Russell   No.

Robin   But you're Mickey's best friend. I understand.

Russell   I don't care about him.

He takes **Robin***'s hand and places it on his crotch.* **Robin** *lunges on him, undoing his jeans.*

Robin   Mickey's so independent, prickly. Yet I see such innocence in your eyes. You want new shoes? I'll take you to the Kings Road, buy you all the shoes you want. Trainers. Jeans. You want special treats? You wanna be my boy?

Russell   I just want . . .

Robin   Can't afford much on your meagre grant.

Russell   I just want someone to look after me.

Mickey   I thought that was my job.

They both jump out of their skin. **Mickey** *has come in silently.* **Russell** *starts to pull his jeans back up.*

Russell   All right Mick?

Robin   Mickey. Darling. Come and join us.

Mickey   No, you're all right.

Russell   Mickey.

Mickey   You carry on. Don't let me stop you.

Robin   Where've you been?

Mickey   Chatting to this bloke back at his squat.

Robin   'Til two in the morning?

Mickey   He's a Socialist Worker.

Robin   And you're a reprobate. A match made in heaven!

Mickey   It's a political thing. Not a job, knobhead.

Russell   Mickey!

Mickey   What?

Russell   Robin's been very generous to us.

Mickey   Yeah and I worked bloody hard for it. Your turn now.

Russell   Why are you being like this?

Mickey   Why do you think Russell?

Russell   Don't tell me you're in love with Robin!

Mickey   How many times? How many times Russell? Have I had to . . . walk you to the toilets in a gay club in case there were blokes trying to look at your cock? How many times have I tried to coax it out of you? You're gay! Like me! But oh no, says Russell. I'm just naturally shy. Not so shy now are you?

Robin   Keep your voice down Mickey.

Russell   I don't know what came over me. I'm not actually . . .

Mickey   See? Even when I find you having sex with a guy you deny it. Or do you only help out when they're busy?

Russell   I'm confused Mickey.

Mickey   Are you darlin'? Well d'you know what Uncle Mickey's going to do for you now?

Russell   Patronise me?

Mickey   He's gonna pack his bags, get out of here and leave you two lovebirds to it. Then maybe you can figure out what you are for yourself.

Russell   You're being ridiculous now.

Mickey   And you're a shithouse. Dunno what you want from life apart from being the world's greatest actor.

Russell   And what's wrong with that?

Mickey   The one profession where it's fine to be a screaming great Mary!

Russell   But I'll never be taken seriously as a leading man!

Mickey   Stand up and be counted Russell! Fight the system. Change it not you.

Russell   You don't know me.

Mickey   I know this much. You're dishonest. About who you are, what you are. That's why you can do this to me. Lying comes easy to you.

Mickey *turns to get his guitar.* **Ellie** *suddenly runs through. She shrieks when she realises there are people there.*

Ellie   Aaaghh! Sorry. I'm looking for Tring town centre.

Russell   Tring?

Ellie   I'm so sorry!

And she is gone. **Russell** *looks to* **Mickey**.

Russell   You didn't see that? That woman?

Mickey   Oh what, hallucinating now are you? (*To* **Robin**.) Have you given him drugs?

Russell   Oh shut up, Mickey. I don't need you.

Mickey   Not as long as there's a mirror in the room, eh darlin'? Nice knowing you Russell. You're on your own now.

Mickey *goes with his guitar.* **Russell** *stews.*

Robin   And then there were two. This is all my fault.

Russell   I think it was about time I cut the apron strings anyway.

Robin   He's so angry all the time.

Russell   Robin? Tell me. About these shoes you're gonna buy me tomorrow. From the Kings Road.

Robin *chuckles. And moves to him. He undoes* **Russell**'s *jeans.*

Russell   Tell me!

Blackout.

Scene Eight – Police station, 1962

Young Tom *comes in and sits in front of his* **Father**, *the Superintendent. He sits at a desk, which has a wastepaper basket beside it. He is currently reading through* **Tom**'s *statement.*

Tom   Father I'm sorry.

Tom's Father   Tom, I've . . . not asked you here as my son, but as a fellow policeman.

Tom   This has brought shame on Mother . . . You . . . The station.

Tom's Father   I've been reading through your statement. This boy. This Billy. One sort of wonders why he came over from Ireland. Maybe he's been in trouble like this before.

Tom   I don't think so. But I promise Father, it'll never happen again.

Tom's Father   It certainly won't. Because we'll make sure that bastard's locked up.

Tom *is thrown by this.*

Tom   But . . . sorry . . . If he's locked up, I'll be locked up. (*Shrugs.*) If that's what you want . . .

Tom's Father   It absolutely isn't what I want. You think I want that shame?

Tom   But . . .

Tom's Father   There was a man once who did things like this. (*He jabs the statement.*) A scientist. Helped us beat Hitler with his clever brain. Took a bloke home he met in a picture house and was arrested for gross indecency. Ring any bells?

Tom *is silent.*

Tom's Father   He was chemically castrated. All the oestrogen they gave him meant he grew breasts. A while back he took a bite of an apple he'd dipped in cyanide. Do you want to end up like him?

Tom   No, Father.

Tom's Father   No, Tom. You want a future with Ellie.

Tom   I'm going to propose to her.

Tom's Father   A career in the force.

Tom   Of course. Of course that's what I want. I'm just not sure it's possible now.

Tom's Father   In life Tom, you will soon begin to realise. Even the impossible can be possible.

Tom   I don't . . .

Tom's Father   Tom, what is the point in you going to prison for something you didn't do? (*Beat.*) Might I trouble you for a light?

Tom *nods and hands him a cigarette lighter.*

Tom's Father   So.

He lights the lighter.

Tom's Father   We are going to take these notes. And do the only thing we can with them.

He sets fire to the papers. He drops them, alight, into the waste paper basket.

Tom's Father   A good fire will cleanse and purify. It will burn the waste away. Now.

He picks up a pen from his desk.

Tom's Father   We are going to take this pen. And start again.

Tom *gulps as his father prepares to rewrite the statement.*

Tom's Father   Tom. Be honest. What choice do you have?

Tom *thinks, then nods.*

Tom   Yes Father.

Blackout.

Scene Nine – Miner's house, 1984

Frank, *a striking Yorkshire miner in his mid-twenties, sits nervously in his living room. Eventually the front door goes. He stands up and his wife* **Sue** *comes in with Mickey's guitar case.*

Frank   Did you get one?

Sue   He's just coming.

Frank   What's he like?

Sue   He's got a cough.

Frank   You've been ages.

Sue   Bus broke down.

Frank   Could you not walk?

Sue   He's got a big bag. And this thing here. (*Indicates guitar.*)

Mickey *comes in with a big overnight bag.*

Mickey   All right?

Sue   This is Frank.

Frank   So you're the bender.

Mickey   Well I'm gay yeah. Nice to meet you mate, all right?

He makes to shake **Frank**'s *hand but* **Frank** *looks to* **Sue** *instead.*

Frank   Have you seen the time?

Mickey   I was the last one to be picked.

Sue   It was like choosing evacuees up there.

Frank   So why were you last?

Mickey   Vegetarian. (*Sneezes.*)

Sue   He dunt eat meat.

Frank   What d'you eat?

Mickey   Anything but meat. D'you mind if I park me 'arris?

He sits.

Frank   No wonder no-one wanted you.

Mickey   Knackered, sorry.

Frank   How comes you took him?

Sue   I got gabbing to Peggy Ollerenshaw on t'way over, all right? So I got there late. After all the good ones had gone. No offence Mickey.

Mickey   (*To* **Frank**.) That's my name. Mickey.

Frank   And you don't eat meat?

Mickey   Meat is murder. D'you know what I mean?

Frank   This whole thing's too frigging weird. We've never had owt like this in the village before.

Mickey   What? Twenty seven lesbians and gay men arriving in convoy?

Mickey *laughs, which brings on a cough.*

Frank   'Ere dunn'e talk funny Sue?

Mickey   I always get ill when I go away. When I went on cub camp I got measles.

Frank   Good miner's cough that.

Sue   D'you need a wash and brush up love?

Mickey   I will before tonight.

Sue   Oh we all will before tonight. Will fish fingers do you for your tea?

Mickey   I don't eat fish. Sorry.

Sue   Only we've not got much in.

Mickey   What were you gonna do them with?

Sue   Peas. Tinned.

Mickey   I'll just have that.

Sue   We ant got much more to offer.

Mickey   S'all right. That's why we're here init.

Frank   So you're going to this disco then?

Mickey   I helped organise it.

Frank   Did you?

Mickey   Yes.

Frank   Why?

Mickey   I was watching the news on the TV. About how the police were treating you all. And I thought there were similarities between. Well. Our community and your community.

Frank   I don't take it up t'shitter. No miner does.

Sue   Fat Barry did. Well he tried to.

Mickey   Margaret Thatcher. She's bad news mate.

Frank   Shake my hand pal.

He holds out his hand and they shake hands, finally.

Sue   Oooh you touched him Frank! He said he want gonna touch you.

Mickey   And when I saw how bad things were for you. I just started collecting money. Set up a group. Lesbians And Gay Men Support The Miners. I've collected over five grand. So I wanted to bring it up to you. In person. Then we had the idea of a disco. If there's one thing us gay boys know. We know how to dance.

Sue   They've got a big coach outside the community centre with that written on it. And a big pink triangle. Right comical it is. We've never seen the likes before in this village. (*Beat.*) I'll put them peas on.

And she exits to the kitchen.

Frank   She's been saving them fish fingers. Wanted to show you this is a good house, with good people.

Mickey   That's my principles. And I won't dilute 'em for anyone. Like you won't.

Frank   Don't come in my house and make out you know me. You don't know how hard this is.

Mickey   I do.

Frank   Fellas are starting to go back. Fed up of hearing their kiddies crying themselves to sleep every night with frigging hunger cramps. Sue spends all day outside the supermarket. Collecting food.

Sue (*off*)   Good for me figure this strike!

Mickey   You've got to keep the faith.

Frank   Yeah? Well faith costs money. And that's summat I've not got. Usually. You strike to make a stand. And to show folk what they're missing. But no-one's missing nowt right now what with Thatcher's stockpiling. So the only folk what are suffering . . . is us.

Sue *returns with a mug of tea for* **Mickey**.

Sue   I bet your Mam and Dad are proud. Peas are on.

Mickey   They're dead. Little orphan Annie. Don't feel sorry for me. They never really got me.

Frank   Coz you're a bender, like?

Mickey   I actually find that word offensive.

Frank   What d'you want me to say then? Homosexual?

Mickey   No. That's so depoliticised. I'm gay.

Sue   I'll send a prayer up to them and tell them how helpful you've been to us.

Frank   So you see you being a . . . gay. As a political thing?

Mickey   We're oppressed. Like you are. Like the working class are. There's a lot of competition to be the nigger of the world right now.

Frank   What have thee and me got in common?

Mickey   I was in a club last night. Twenty coppers come in and just started arresting people or beating them up. No reason. They weren't doing nothing. Dancing. Drinking. Just enjoying themselves. I managed to leg it, but . . .

He lets the words settle.

Frank   You play guitar?

Mickey   Yeah.

Frank   Give us a song then.

Mickey   I don't usually have a go til I've had a drink.

Sue   There's a brew. Sing.

Mickey *gets the guitar out and starts to pluck.*

Frank   You be all right kipping on t'couch?

Mickey   Well if you can't be arsed to give up your four poster for the likes of me . . .

Frank   I don't leave my bed for any bugger. Especially not a bugger like thee.

They share a smile. Eventually **Mickey** *starts to sing.*

Mickey (*sings*)
    This government had an idea
    And parliament made it law
    It seems like it's illegal
    To fight for the union any more
    Which side are you on, boys?
    Which side are you on?
    Which side are you on, boys?
    Which side are you on?

We set out to join the picket line
For together we cannot fail
We got stopped by police at the county line
They said, "Go home boys or you're going to jail"

Which side are you on, boys?
Which side are you on?
Which side are you on, boys?
Which side are you on?

It's hard to explain to a crying child
Why her Daddy can't go back
So the family suffer
But it hurts me more
To hear a scab say Sod you, Jack

Which side are you on, boys?
Which side are you on?
Which side are you on, boys
Which side are you on?

As he dissolves in a coughing fit.

Blackout.

Scene Ten – Courtroom, 1962

Billy *is in the dock. The* **Judge** *is addressing him.*

Judge   William James Lynch. You have been found guilty
of the most heinous of crimes. That on the afternoon of
June 13th of this year you procured Thomas Ian Harris back
to your bedsit on Addison Road, Wavertree, where you
attacked him in the most lewd and offensive manner
imaginable. This was a shocking case. At many points in the
trial, as you know, I had to ask ladies to leave the court . . .
fearful as I was for their constitution. Thomas Ian Harris is
a young policeman of fine reputation, impeccable character,
and with a great career ahead of him doing good for the
people of Liverpool. On June the thirteenth you tried to

put a stop to that by perverting him. By your own admission you are a homosexualist.

Billy   I am Sir, yes.

Judge   An amazing admission. But Mr Lynch. I am going to do something that will surprise you now. I am going to take pity on you.

Billy   I don't want your pity Sir. There's nothing wrong with me.

Judge   No interrupting, please!

Billy   But there isn't!

Judge   Silence! Or I'll have you for contempt of court. Now. I am going to give you two options. You are not happy being a homosexualist?

Billy   I don't like the pain it's caused my family, no Sir. But . . .

Judge   It was a rhetorical question. And therefore I offer you this. Three years in prison. Or. You go directly from here to the Lancashire Centre for Psychiatric Treatment where you will have your disease cured.

Billy   How do they cure it?

Judge   Which is it to be?

Billy   How? I don't want to go to prison, but . . .

Judge   Excellent. You strike me as a decent man Mr Lynch. Let's see if we can't make you a normal man. Recite the Lord's Prayer five times.

Billy   I beg your pardon?

Judge   The Lord's Prayer. Someone has to pray for your soul, man.

Pause.

Billy   Our Father, who art in heaven. Hallowed be thy name. Thy Kingdom come, thine will be done, on earth as it is in heaven. Give us this day our daily bread, and forgive us our trespasses.

And he keeps praying, the set changes, bringing us to . . .

Scene Eleven – Hospital room, 1984

Mickey lies in a sparse hospital side room. A sign above his bed reads BARRIER NURSING. He lies in silence for a while. After a while he calls out.

Mickey   Hello?

No response. No-one comes.

Mickey   Hello?

Silence.

Mickey   I'd like water.

*It is hard for him to shout as his throat is sore. He continues to lie there. A **Nurse** comes in dressed in what looks like a space suit. Goggles, hat, gloves, mask, white coat, like something from a horror movie. She carries a tray with a glass of water on it. She walks slowly to the bed and places the tray on the floor nearby. She walks slowly away.*

Mickey   I don't bite.

*The **Nurse** looks back.*

Nurse   You might spit at me.

Mickey   But I won't.

*The **Nurse** turns and carries on walking. **Mickey** lies there. Eventually he tries to sit up. This action is difficult. Very slowly he sits. He can't reach the water.*

Mickey   Hello? Please. I can't . . . Hello?

But no-one comes.

Blackout.

Scene Twelve – Psychiatric hospital, 1962/Hospital, 1984

Billy *lies in an iron bed drinking a bottle of Guinness. A crate of Guinness lies beside the bed. A psychiatrist,* **Dr McKinnon,** *sits nearby in a chair.*

Billy I didn't attack him.

Dr McKinnon What did you do?

Billy We made love.

Dr McKinnon Interesting way of describing it.

Billy If I'd attacked him would he have kissed me?

Dr McKinnon You kiss?

Billy Would he have sung to me?

Dr McKinnon What other things do you do with men?

Billy Talk?

Dr McKinnon Sexually.

Billy It's private.

Dr McKinnon D'you suck their penises? (*Pause.*) It's a straightforward enough question William. Do you suck their penises?

Billy It's private.

Dr McKinnon D'you want to suck my penis?

Billy No.

Dr McKinnon Do you become aroused when I talk about this penis business?

Billy No.

Dr McKinnon Sure?

He moves and puts his hand over **Billy**'s *crotch.* **Billy** *tenses.*

Dr McKinnon And relax.

Billy *lies back.* **Dr McKinnon** *removes his hand.*

Dr McKinnon   Have another drink. Guinness. Your favourite.

Billy   Why are you letting me drink?

Dr McKinnon   The drug I administer reacts with it.

Billy   In what way? What's gonna happen to me?

Dr McKinnon   Five minutes from now you'll be vomiting profusely and have crippling diarrhoea. It's all good.

Pause.

So. William.

Billy   Dr McKinnon. Sir. My name's Billy.

Dr McKinnon   Billy. To cure you of your sickness we need to get to the heart of what the sickness is. So in order to do that I need you to tell me what you do with these men. You do know that if you refuse treatment you'll be sent away. You don't want to do that. This is for your own good. You are a dirty, filthy queer. Now you can't change that of your own free will, but I can. I can change you Billy. Do you want to be changed?

Billy   I'm . . .

Dr McKinnon   It'll only take a matter of days.

Billy   I'm scared.

Dr McKinnon   It's . . . just like a visit to the dentist. Relax, Billy.

And he approaches him and injects him.

Dr McKinnon   Have another drink, Billy. Go on, that's right. Have a nice drink.

Billy has a drink. And immediately feels ill.

Dr McKinnon   Okay now I want you to put the headphones on and look at the screen.

Billy *puts a pair of headphones on and looks to the screen. The lights dim. On the screen we see a slide show of various naked and semi naked men. The tape starts to play. We hear voices whispering at first, then getting louder. Its* **Dr McKinnon**'s *voice amplified and echoing.* **Dr McKinnon** *straps* **Billy** *into the bed so he can't move.*

Dr McKinnon   Dirty filthy queer. Dirty filthy queer. Dirty filthy cock sucking queer.

Billy *starts to be sick over himself.*

Billy   Please can I have a bucket?

And he is sick again.

Dr McKinnon   The screen Billy. Look at the screen.

The voices get louder as **Billy** *continues to be sick. He is crying now. The voices echo around us. Under it we hear* **Tom**, *singing, and he appears in shadow at the back of the stage, singing mournfully.*

Tom   If you're fond of sand dunes and salty air
Quaint little villages here and there
You're bound to fall in love with old Cape Cod.

He walks across the stage having a late night cigarette.

Tom   If you like the taste of a lobster stew
Served by a window with an ocean view
You're sure to fall in love with old Cape Cod.

Tom *exits as the noises get louder and louder. Deafening.* **Billy**'s *pain growing.* **Dr McKinnon** *staring on blankly. Just then the noise stops and the lights come up on the hospital where* **Mickey** *has fallen out of bed.* **Russell** *rushes in.*

Russell   Jesus, are you all right?

Mickey   Well you took your fucking time!

Blackout.

Act Two

Scene One – Tom's living room, 2010.

Tom *stands alone, the guilt about the aversion therapy weighing heavily upon him.* **Russell** *comes in, slurping from a glass of red.*

Russell I've just been to the loo. Your wife's in her room. Staring into space. Curiosity got the better of me. Had a bit of a nose about. Lots of photos. On the walls. But no evidence of any . . . sordid little secrets. No pictures of him. Made your mind up yet?

Tom Don't judge me.

Russell I like Melanie. She reminds me of someone.

Tom Have you told her?

Russell I'm going to. I have to.

Tom You don't know how lucky you are.

Russell You don't know the first thing about me.

Tom I see you in magazines. All beaming smiles while you show us the contents of your fridge. Like we're interested.

Russell And do the contents of your cupboards show the extent of your existential pain, Tom? Well I guess your closet does.

Tom It was easier for you.

Russell Easy? In the eighties and nineties we were decimated. Oh yeah, that's a piece of piss!

Tom Well you did all right! And at least it was legal!

Russell You should've known it was right!

Tom So says the voice of privilege. Out there in the spotlight while we were forced to hide in the shadows.

Russell And you're still there. What's wrong with a bit of light? The things you're hiding might not look so bad.

Tom   And how many people would that hurt?

Russell   Your lies have hurt me. Your lies have hurt him.

Tom   I know it was you, tipped the press off. What did you say? Tom Harris is a faggot? Nail him?

Russell   If it had been me, Mr P.C. Self Pity, I wouldn't've started with that particular story.

Tom   Well you know more than you're letting on.

Russell   I told you. I know journalists.

Tom   You know showbiz journalists, presumably. What? One of them tipped you off about a political hot potato? So you came rushing round to give me the heads up? It doesn't make sense.

Russell   Who told the press is really not the issue here.

Tom   Or is it a form of Munchausen's? Offering me the support so you can watch me suffer and make yourself an integral character in my little drama.

Russell   I'm not doing this for you! I'm doing this for him!

Tom   I've watched you rise to the top and felt an almost paternal pride. But now I've seen you again . . .

Russell   You're not honouring him!

Tom   And have you never done anything you're not proud of?

Russell   Tom! Don't make this about me. Please. Do the right thing. For the first time.

Tom   And it's that straightforward, is it?

Russell *despairs. The lights rise on:*

Scene Two – B and B, 1962

Billy *sits, shell shocked, on the bed of a modest B and B.* **Tom** *comes in.*

Tom   The bath's running.

Billy   Thank you.

Tom   It's a nice B and B.

Billy   I know.

Tom   I told them I was bringing my brain damaged cousin from Ireland for a treat. Thought they wouldn't question a double bed then.

Billy *nods. Shocked. After a while.*

Tom   I was gonna get you to shuffle a bit, but . . . You seemed to do that automatically. What did they do to you in there?

Billy   It's so quiet here. Wasn't there. All hours of the night. Never silent. People's fear.

Tom   I've not been sleeping too good either.

Billy   You stood up in a court of law and said I'd attacked you. Me, who wouldn't harm a hair on your head. I lay for three days in my own piss and shit. That's not the cosiest mattress in the world. You excuse me as your brain damaged brother, I'm not surprised you don't sleep so fucking good.

Tom   You've changed.

Billy   I believe that was the idea.

Tom   D'you like girls now?

Billy *starts to cry.* **Tom** *moves close and hugs him.*

Billy   I feel so dirty. Please can I have a bath?

Tom   Come on. Let's get you undressed.

Tom *starts to take* **Billy***'s clothes off.*

Billy   Say nice things to me.

Tom   Like what?

Billy   What have you been up to?

Tom   Can I kiss you Billy?

Billy   After my bath.

Tom   You don't smell.

Billy   I can smell him.

Tom   Who?

Billy   And after. We can stay here forever. And nobody need ever know.

Tom   Might be a bit of a problem. I'm getting married on Saturday.

Pause. **Billy** *is taken aback.*

Billy   I hope you'll be very happy together.

Tom   You always knew it'd be on the cards.

Billy   You bastard Tom!

Tom   Billy.

Billy   Bringing me here? Getting my hopes up? D'you know what? I wish I had attacked you.

Tom   Don't say that!

Billy   Why not? It's true. Explain to me in words of one syllable or more what's good about my life. My future. There's nothing.

Tom   I'd be angry if I was you. I am angry. I'd hate me.

Billy   And you know the pathetic thing? I don't. Explain that in words of one syllable or more. So you see they were right. I did want locking up. Certifiable. I want me head testing. And guess what. It was. They stuck electrodes in my head while I looked at pictures of you. And the sickest bit of all was . . . All along, I hoped you'd be waiting for me.

Billy *heads for the bathroom. He walks with difficulty.*

Tom   I'll wash your back Billy.

Billy   Go back to Ellie, Tom. See if she'll let you rub her back.

Tom   Please.

Billy   Leave me alone Tom. You've fucked me up.

Tom   You're not gonna do anything daft are you?

Billy   Like what? Drown myself? Interesting question though, loverboy. What do I do now? Sink or swim?

He stands at the bathroom door.

Blackout.

Scene Three – Private room, House of Commons, 1986

Russell *rushes on dressed as a waiter, black trousers and a dickie bow, which isn't fastened properly. A woman follows him in,* **Mrs Ford**. *She is dressed as a waitress and is carrying a tray with canapés on it.*

Mrs Ford   You're late, Russell!

Russell   I'm sorry Mrs Ford! I won't let it happen again!

Mrs Ford   You certainly won't or you'll be out on your ear.

Russell   I had to be somewhere and it took longer than I thought.

Mrs Ford   Have you been crying Mr Dowler?

Russell   No, I get hay fever.

Mrs Ford   I think men who cry are poofters. I only chose you because you're usually so reliable and polite.

Russell   I won't let you down, Mrs Ford.

She hands him the tray as **Margaret Thatcher** *and* **Norman Fowler** *enter, completely ignoring their presence.* **Mrs Ford** *scurries out, dropping a curtsy to* **Margaret** *as she goes.* **Margaret** *is reading a document.* **Norman** *waits patiently for her to finish it. The document fills her with some disgust.* **Russell** *steps forward and offers his tray to them, they ignore it.*

Margaret   It is surely impossible to gain pleasure from several of these practices. If not all.

She continues to read.

Norman   Well. The research shows . . .

Margaret   And where do you propose to display this information?

Norman   This is a press campaign Prime Minister.

Margaret   Newspapers are very public Norman.

Norman   The public is who we're trying to reach, Prime Minister.

Margaret   Better, surely, to put this up on toilet walls. Like information about V.D.

Norman   It's vital we reach as many people as possible. This is a life and death battle. And we the government can do something to determine the outcome. I don't want people to look back in five years time and say 'If only they'd done more in 1986'.

Margaret   Oral sex?

She shakes her head in disbelief.

Norman   I know. I had no idea you could get it from talking dirty.

He sniggers. She sees something in the document which turns her stomach. She wretches.

Norman   I have two messages Prime Minister. Do not inject drugs, but if you cannot stop, do not share equipment. And secondly. Stick to one sexual partner, but if you do not, use a condom.

Margaret   The wording.

Norman   Which wording, Prime Minister?

Margaret   Where to start? Condom. No. Say sheath.

Norman   Sheath?

Margaret   Yes, sheath. Do you need me to spell it for you?

Norman   No, of course not.

Margaret   I don't like 'anal intercourse'.

Norman   What would you prefer?

Margaret   What about 'back passage intercourse'?

Pause. Eventually **Norman** *takes up a pen and makes notes.*

Norman   Back passage . . .

Margaret   No. Even better. Rectal sex. Is this really necessary?

Norman   The people we are trying to speak to indulge in these bizarre behaviours. And . . . rectal sex spreads the virus more than sex in the vagina.

And he pronounces vagina wrong. **Margaret** *takes a canapé off* **Russell***'s tray.*

Norman   The membranes in the rectum are thinner, therefore more easy to tear.

Margaret   Thank you Norman.

Norman   Whereas in the vagina . . .

And he pronounced it wrong again.

Margaret   Norman please. I'm eating.

Norman   I'm sorry.

Margaret   And you would do very well to remember you are more than just the Minister for AIDS.

Norman   I would rather have some people offended by our content than many people dying. We're acting for the public good.

Margaret   Will that be all Norman?

Russell   Ma'am? Ma'am? . . .

Margaret *looks to him. He wants to say something. He struggles, but then bottles it.*

Russell   Another canapé Ma'am?

Margaret   No.

Norman   Can we hurry this campaign up? Something like this usually takes two, maybe three months to organise, but in that time I dread to think how many deaths we'll have . . .

Margaret   Perspective, Norman. This is not a big problem. People who get AIDS. It is entirely their fault. Their responsibility, their choice. Let's not lose too much sleep over them.

Norman   I disagree.

Margaret   You are wrong. People today are being taught that they have an inalienable right to be gay. We must stop this.

Norman   So you won't hurry the campaign up?

Margaret   No.

Norman   Thank you, Prime Minister.

And she heads for the door. She stops and turns back.

Margaret   Oh and Norman.

Norman   Prime Minister?

Margaret   It's vagina.

He exits. **Margaret** *becomes aware of* **Russell***'s hand shaking the tray of canapés.*

Blackout.

Scene Four – Hospital room, 1986

Mickey, *sitting up in bed, is livid. He is weaker than last we saw him. But has not lost any of his fight.* **Russell** *sits at the end of the bed.*

Mickey   I don't believe you. I do not . . .

Russell   Try not to get worked up.

Mickey   You had her sat there. Inches away from you. You could've touched her. Maimed her. And you didn't say anything? Russell you amaze me. Surely you can't still be a closet queen? Or worse still, a Tory.

Russell   I'm not anything. I refuse to be pigeon holed.

Mickey   You could at least have punched her. For me, if not for you. Or poisoned her. Or . . .

Russell   I'm only doing silver service waiting till . . .

Mickey   She was sat there talking about AIDS and you never said nothing?

Russell   Anything.

Mickey   Call yourself gay? You're not gay. You're a homosexual!

Russell   I was upset, okay?

Mickey   I thought we was sisters. Blood brothers.

Russell   We are.

Mickey   So how could you just stand there like she was Joe Anybody?

Russell   Okay, so maybe I'm changing my mind about politics.

Mickey   If you are going to be a Tory, at least own up to it. I'd have more respect for you then, if you were just honest. Honest about something.

Russell   I was having a bad day.

Mickey   Oh you're having a bad day. You're having a bad day.

Russell   Well I was!

Mickey   Put yourself in my shoes. See how you like this.

Russell   I was putting myself in your shoes actually. Maybe we are blood brothers. In more ways than one. I didn't wanna tell you but I've gotta tell someone. Before I burst.

Pause. But now he wants to say it, **Russell** *finds he hasn't got the words.* **Mickey***'s face crumbles. Just then the* **Nurse** *comes in, slightly less covered up now, carrying food on a tray.*

Nurse   Morning Mickey. Soup of the day. Chicken and tarragon. Try and eat your bread.

She places it on the bed.

Nurse   Bon appétit.

They wait for her to retreat.

Mickey   Russell.

Russell   I can't say it. I can't say the words.

Mickey   What can't you say baby?

Russell   I don't wanna say it. If I say it it's real. And then I won't be able to cope.

Mickey   No. No. No! You can't get ill.

Russell   You better eat your food.

Mickey   You gotta be strong for me. It's your turn now. It's your turn to care for me. I've got no-one else.

Russell   Eat your crusts. Make your hair curly.

Mickey   Russell look at me!

Russell *turns and shrugs.*

Russell   It's all right for you. You'll go first. Who's gonna look after me?

Mickey   You have to copy everything I do.

Russell   You go on all the adventures. I get left behind.

Mickey   Oh this is an awfully big adventure. The biggest.

Russell   I don't wanna be left behind. But I don't wanna go neither.

Mickey   Either.

Russell *smiles.*

Mickey (*Sings*)   Remember me as a sunny day
That you once had along the way
Remember me as a breath of spring
Remember me as a good thing.

Russell   I have a recall.

Mickey   For what?

Russell   Second cast of *Les Misérables*. It's this musical that's coming into the West End. About a load of miserable French people.

Mickey *rolls his eyes.*

Mickey   Great.

Russell   I come on in full drag on the barricades and sing this show-stopping number called 'Let Them Eat Cake'.

Mickey *is tearful.*

Russell   I don't really.

Mickey *smiles.*

Mickey   I wish you would. I wish you'd be proud.

Russell   I don't know if it's worth me going. I could be dead within a week.

Mickey   Yes but you could die onstage. You have to do it.

Russell   I just keep wanting to wash myself. I look at my hands and . . . they're not my hands any more.

Mickey   How's Robin?

Russell   I moved out. I'm sorry Mickey. About . . .

Mickey   Hey. I've got you back now. That's all that matters.

They lie there together, on his bed, staring into space.

Scene Five – Ellie's house, 1962

Young Ellie *stands in her wedding dress. She sings to herself. Linden Lea. As she sings, older* **Ellie** *comes in and watches her, eventually joining in.*

Young Ellie   Within the woodlands, flow'ry gladed,
                     By the oak trees' mossy moot,
                     The shining grass blades, timber-shaded,
                     Now do quiver underfoot;
                     And birds do whistle overhead,
                     And water's bubbling in its bed,

Both Ellies   And there, for me, the apple tree
                     Do lean down low in Linden Lea.

Young Ellie *suddenly notices her and stops singing.*

Young Ellie   Who are you?

Ellie   A concerned party.

Young Ellie   You must be on Mother's side. You look like her.

Ellie   You have a beautiful voice.

Young Ellie   The choir are going to sing that. What d'you want? You should really be getting to the church.

Ellie   I've . . . come to show you these.

She passes her a pile of letters, wrapped in a blue satin ribbon.

Ellie   You find them. In a few year's time. You think you're really clever opening out the chimney in the box room.

Young Ellie *unfurls the ribbon and reads the first letter.*

Ellie   By then you feel it's old news. He's changed. He's a different man. He's not.

Young Ellie   This is Tom's handwriting.

Ellie   Billy turns up. At the wedding. He's probably there now. You're walking down the aisle with Tom. Newly married. And there he is. Up in the gallery. And he drops these. So many letters. Raining down on you. Tom rushes to pick them up. You ask him what they are. He's evasive. He's always evasive.

Young Ellie   Billy's an invert. A trouble maker. He attacked Tom.

Ellie   The letters show that's just not true. I believe the French is billet doux. It sounds so much less hurtful in French.

Young Ellie   I like French. I wanted to study it at University. But Mam says I should marry and settle down. Have children. I really want children. Children respect their parents. Love them.

Ellie   It's rarely that straightforward. Don't go. It's not too late to back out.

Young Ellie   I don't know who you are. And I don't believe these letters. Tom's a good man. He loves me.

Ellie   When the letters rain down. And Tom's evasive, you'll know.

Young Ellie   Who are you?

Ellie   Can't you see Ellie? I'm you.

Young Ellie   You're dead old. And you speak dead posh.

Ellie   We move away from Liverpool.

Young Ellie   No. I'm never gonna leave Liverpool. My family. Tom'd never take me away from them. You're off your cake you!

Ellie   Was I really this feisty?

Young Ellie   I'm pregnant. We've got to marry.

Ellie   When it's raining letters. You'll know.

Young Ellie (*handing the letters back*)   If you're me, you'll understand why I have to do this.

Ellie (*nods and helps her on with her veil*)   You'll never look more beautiful.

She kisses her and goes. The lights rise on:

Scene Six – Theatre 1987 / Church 1962

Ellie *appears in her wedding dress and veil. She walks down the aisle to the front of the church, alone, to the music.* **Tom** *appears at the other end of the church, in his wedding suit, checking his buttonhole.*

Russell *stands up on the bed. He is onstage performing in* Les Misérables.

Russell   Will you join in our crusade?
           Who will be strong and stand with me?
           Beyond the barricade, is there a world you long to see?
           Then join in the fight that will give you the right to be free.
           Do you hear the people sing?
           Singing the songs of angry men?

It is the music of a people who will not be slaves again
When the beating of your heart, echoes the beating of the drums

There is a life about to start when tomorrow comes

As he sings it starts to rain letters. **Tom***'s love letters fall down on* **Ellie** *and* **Tom**. *They look up as the lights fade. As they do a phone starts to ring.*

Scene Seven – Festival of Light offices, 1971

Mary Whitehouse *standing in her office on the phone.*

Mary   Hello, Festival of Light? (*Beat.*) Cliff Richard as I live and breathe! How's my favourite popster? (*Beat.*) I'm wonderful thank you dear, if not a little overexcited about Thursday. Are you all geared up to show the world how much we abhor homosexuality? Prostitution? All that jazz? (*Beat.*) Of course.

(*She covers the receiver and calls, off*)

William!! (*on phone*) My new Man Friday. Been working in the office for a while now.

Billy *comes running in with a clipboard.*

Billy   Yes Mrs Whitehouse?

Mary   What time is lovely Cliff being picked up on Thursday?

Billy *checks his clipboard.*

Billy   Nine forty Mrs Whitehouse.

Mary   Twenty to ten dear. Is that all right? Lovely. (*Beat.*) You too Cliff. See you Thursday. And say a prayer that everything runs as smoothly as possibly. Bye now. (*Hangs up. To* **Billy**.) But of course with you as my side that's hardly necessary.

Billy   Mrs Whitehouse, was that really Cliff Richard?

Mary   Yes dear.

Billy   Wow. Does he hate homosexuals too?

Mary   He pities them. He hates what they do. There is a difference.

Billy   But d'you know what Mrs Whitehouse? Sometimes I thank God for homosexuals and pornographers because it gives you the ammunition to get out there and kick ass!

Mary   Well that's . . . very kind of you to say so William but please. No Americanisms here.

Billy   Oh I'm just passionate, Mrs Whitehouse. I can't wait to alert society to moral pollution. Raise spiritual standards. Spread evangelical Christianity. All that jazz.

Mary   So. Run me through the transport arrangements for Thursday will you?

Billy   Cliff Richard you know about. We also have cars booked for Malcolm Muggeridge, Lord Longford, the Bishop and your good self. Car parking information for central London has been sent out to every single church in the country. Every ticket has been sold and. .

Mary   My beacons?

Billy   A chain of beacons will be lit through the country to shine a light into moral pollution.

Mary   Shall I put the kettle on William? Make us both a nice strong cup of tea?

Billy   Heavenly.

Mary   You do say the funniest things.

She exits. He turns the page on his clipboard and clears his throat . . .

Billy   Opening ceremony. Enter the hall in small groups. Dress conservatively. Act unobtrusively. Make no sign of protest until it is your turn. Do not speak to each other. Let the previous group's demonstration end before yours begins. Let everything settle down and the speeches start again. Our purpose is to slow down and delay proceedings. Stick to your agreed form of protest and do so clearly and loudly. Offer passive resistance only. Do not fight back. Let Operation Rupert commence!

He turns and calls, off.

Billy   Oh Mrs Whitehouse. I'm so excited about Thursday. I think it's going to be a day to remember!

Blackout.

Scene Eight – Hospital, 1986

Mickey *lies in bed, incredibly ill now.* **Russell** *sits one side. A* **Nurse** *is applying make-up to* **Mickey**'s *face to cover his lesions.*

Russell   I know that one day I'll wake up and find that the virus has come and attacked me. I just get so bored of waiting. I wanna scream out. Attack me now you bastard! I'm ready for you!!

Nurse   Oh. I found another clipping for his collection. John Junor in the Mail on Sunday.

She hands it to **Russell**.

Russell   (*reads*) Dear Diana. Do you really want to go down in history as the Patron Saint of Sodomy?

Nurse   I was quite proud of myself, finding that one.

Russell   Some days I just know it's here. Sore throat. Shortness of breath. Red rash when I shave. Red rash when I don't shave. I bruise easily, so thin skin. A tendency to feel the cold. A tendency to feel the heat. Tiredness. Anxiety. Panic attacks on tubes. A fear of confined spaces. The inability to see in the dark.

Nurse   Not that you're self obsessed or anything.

Russell   A tendency to yawn when nurses are dull. KS.

Nurse   Have you got KS?

Russell   Name that tumour.

He very quickly lifts his top.

Nurse   It's a bruise.

Russell   I know. I know. I should get a life other than eight shows a week and coming here. But what else can I do? Look at him.

Mickey   He's fine.

Russell   She walks, she talks, she's a freakin' miracle!

Mickey   What were you talking about?

Russell   The view from this window. Stunning. Shame you're blind really.

Mickey   Piss off.

Russell   Oh forgive me. You're not blind, your retinas have become detached. I'm sorry.

Mickey   I can still tell you're ugly.

Nurse   We've gotta get you better so we can get you out for Thursday.

She hands him a mirror.

Nurse   I've covered it up quite well. Now you can greet your public.

Mickey   Thursday? What's . . .

Russell   Robin's funeral's Thursday.

Mickey   Robin?

Russell   We told you last night. Don't you remember? God, your memory!

Mickey   Of course, of course I rember.

Russell   They're dropping like flies. Every day a different name. Joe on Tuesday. Lee on Wednesday. Mark on . . .

Mickey   Is this it then? He was diagnosed two weeks before me. Have I got two weeks left then?

Russell   It doesn't work like that.

Mickey   How do you know? You're not a doctor.

Russell   But we're the fucking experts here. I don't like that any more than you do but we are.

Mickey   Two weeks. Bollocks. Well you know what this means.

Russell   It might mean nothing.

Mickey   You're gonna have to call my Mum and Dad.

Nurse   I thought they were dead.

Russell   He's prone to exaggeration. They're just a little bit dull and a tad homophobic. They're also perenially middle class. That Billericay accent? It's all an act.

Mickey   Time to resurrect them.

Russell   What do I say? Mickey, what do I say?

Mickey   'You know your son Michael? He's got a touch of the AIDS about him'. Drama queen.

Russell   Piss off!

Mickey   Read me my clippings.

Russell *gets a plastic bag off the bed and pulls out some cuttings from newspapers.*

Russell   Right, this is from *The Sun*. And it says 'Straight Sex Cannot Give You AIDS'. Official.

Mickey   The breeders are so blessed.

They all laugh.

Russell   'Robert Simpson, a vicar from Barmston in Humberside has vowed to take his eighteen year old son Russell – ah! My namesake! – vowed to take his son to a mountain and shoot him if he develops AIDS.

Nurse   Oh he sounds lovely.

Mickey   Dicky Divine!

Russell   'Russell would never get closer to me than six yards' says Simpson. 'He would be a dead man. And that would go for the rest of my family, and strangers.'

A chill descends in the room. They can't be bothered to joke about it any more.

Russell   When asked what he thought, Russell replied, 'I sometimes think he'd like to shoot me whether I had AIDS or not.'

Nurse   Is anyone else cold?

The lights fade.

Scene Nine – Down by the railway line, Billericay, 1971

It's night. It's pouring with rain. **Young Tom** *comes on with a torch, soaked to the skin, looking for something.*

Young Tom   Son? Can you hear me? Can you hear me lad? Are you there?!

Presently **Young Ellie** *comes on carrying an umbrella and shining another torch.* **Tom** *appears in the shadows, watching them.*

Young Ellie   Tom? Tom?

Young Tom   Over here!

Young Ellie   Tom he's safe. He's home. One of the neighbours found him!

Young Tom   Where?

Young Ellie   They'd told him there were monsters at the bottom of their garden, he'd gone looking for them.

Young Tom   In the pouring rain?!

Young Ellie   He said it was an adventure. He could've caught his death Tom! I leave him with you for one hour . . .

Young Tom   I was showing Steve from next door the Datsun Cherry.

Young Ellie   Why didn't you notice he'd gone?

Young Tom   We were in the garage.

Young Ellie   I don't like Steve. Tom your shirt's ripped.

Young Tom   Yeah I fell over.

She takes his hand.

Young Ellie   Have you been in a fight?

Young Tom   Don't be daft.

Young Ellie   You've ruined my night. Putting the fear of God into me. It was so embarrassing at the Tupperware party, when you called. I could've died.

Young Tom   I'm dying Ellie. Every time I step foot through the door. I see monsters at the bottom of our garden.

Young Ellie   It's called married life, Tom. I don't see why you think you've got a right to be any happier than the rest of us.

Young Tom   I don't love you Ellie.

Young Ellie   Get a backbone Tom!

She hurries off, heading home.

Young Tom   Sweet Jesus, when will it ever end?

*Suddenly **Tom** steps out of the shadows.*

Tom   Tonight?

Young Tom   Keep away from me. Keep away from me!

And he backs away into the shadows.

Scene Ten – Mount Ararat, 2010

*It's night. The swirling mists at the top of Ararat. Through the fog we find **Ellie** reaching the summit, shining a torch to light the way. A **Vicar** is sitting on a pile of clothes, waiting, with a machine gun, lit by a camp fire. It is raining heavily.*

Ellie That's . . . quite some climb. What is this place?

Vicar Ararat. Mount. The world's drowning.

Ellie Where God started again.

Vicar I'd prefer not to converse 'til the Ark gets here.

Ellie Do you mind if I sit? My legs aren't what they were.

He shrugs. She joins him.

Ellie I looked for Tring. Couldn't find it. Tried to change my destiny. I failed. (*Gasps.*) Oh! You have a gun!

Vicar No sudden movements.

Ellie Can I ask you something?

Vicar You might wake my son.

*The **Vicar** suddenly shoots the gun. **Ellie** screams and jumps out of the way.*

Vicar I saw something move.

Ellie You see, the thing is I went to church. Every Sunday for twenty years. I sometimes took my son when I needed to practice the organ. He'd play in the church and I'd tap and pedal away. He used to sit on the carpet and say 'Mum. Come and sit on here and we can go on a magic carpet ride'. I used to tell him not to be so silly. How I wish I'd joined him. I wore this coat. My Sunday coat. He said it made me look like the Queen. I burnt it when he died. (*Beat.*) Your son?

Vicar (*nods*) You can help me dispose of the body.

She looks to him alarmed. She realises she is sitting on his son's corpse.

Ellie Is this him?

And she taps him.

Vicar Don't hit him.

Ellie You shot him!

Vicar   Well he had the disease.

Ellie   Did he?

Vicar   Yes! Well I don't know actually.

Ellie   So why did you . . .

Vicar   It was so hard to tell in the eighties.

Ellie   Will you tell me if Jesus forgives me?

Vicar   What did you do wrong?

Ellie   I committed the worst crime. I turned my back on my son.

Vicar   I killed mine. There were extenuating circumstances.

Ellie   There should be no excuses. (*Stands.*) Okay. I know what I have to do. I don't think the ark is coming. I think it's been and gone.

She heads off. Suddenly the wind gets up and mists swirl more, enclosing them. When eventually the fog separates we find:

Scene Eleven – Hospital, 1986

Mickey *is sitting up in bed.* **Russell** *is brushing his hair.*

Russell   I'm shaking. Why am I nervous?

Mickey   Coz you're a big fat Jessie.

Russell   They're your bloody parents. Let's have a look.

He steps back to admire his handiwork.

Russell   You don't look too bad.

Mickey   Thanks.

Russell   Okay you look brilliant.

Mickey   I don't care how I look. The more shocking the better.

Russell   Where are they? The nurse said they were at the entrance ten minutes ago.

Mickey   Probably got lost.

Russell   Come out of the wrong lift and currently partaking in a Popmobility class. Aaand stretch! Where are they?

He hurries to the door and looks out.

Russell   I think I see them. Do I curtsy?

Mickey   Calm down.

Tom *and* **Ellie** *come in.* **Ellie** *is wearing a coat that wouldn't look out of place on the Queen.* **Tom** *has a bouquet of flowers.* **Ellie** *freezes in the doorway.*

Russell (*Nods.*)   Mr Harris. Mrs Harris.

Tom (*To* **Mickey.**)   Hello Son.

Mickey   I'm blind. Prove it's you.

Ellie *remains frozen as* **Tom** *approaches the bed. He sits at* **Mickey**'s *side.*

Tom   You know it's me.

Mickey   When I was little. Mum's birthday party. I was in bed and I heard you singing in the garden. I pulled the curtains back and saw you. I thought you'd be singing to Mum. But you were singing to the stars. If you can remember that song, it's you.

Tom *clears his throat and eventually starts to sing.*

Tom   If you're fond of sand dunes and salty air
          Quaint little villages here and there
          You're bound to fall in love with old Cape Cod.

He goes to take **Mickey**'s *hand but can't.* **Ellie** *remains in the doorway.* **Mickey** *cries.*

Russell   You can come in Mrs Harris.

She doesn't budge.

Ellie   Did you give it to him?

Russell   What? No. I love him very much Mrs Harris. He's my best friend.

Ellie   Is this what love does?

Ellie *looks away.* **Russell** *goes and looks out of the window.*

Tom   If you like the taste of a lobster stew
Served by a window with an ocean view
You're sure to fall in love with old Cape Cod.

As he sings, **Melanie** *walks in with older* **Russell**. *They survey the tableau. She is shocked. She looks to* **Russell**.

Melanie   I live on my nerves. I'm by nature a very nervous person.

Russell *nods. She looks to* **Ellie**.

Melanie   So much for the Moped in Tring.

The lights fade.

Act Three

Scene One – Central Hall, 1971

Lights up on **Mary Whitehouse** *standing at a lectern addressing the Festival of Life Gathering. During the scene, various actors will be placed in the audience to disrupt her talk. Mostly men in drag, dressed up as Home Counties Housewives.*

Mary Ladies and Gentlemen. Friends. Christians. Welcome to Central Hall in the heart of Westminster for the very first Festival of Light in this the year of our Lord, 1971. We're here today to celebrate everything that's wonderful and bounteous about our existence. And hopefully to shine some of our light in the murky tunnels and under stones that others would rather leave unturned.

Someone in the audience starts to slow clap. It unnerves **Mary**. *The clapping gets louder, spreading.*

Mary I have some friends who recently returned from a year abroad as Missionaries. Peter and Janet Hill. And what were they confronted with? The Oz trial. Ken Russell's film *The Devils*. The growth of open homosexuality. Women's Lib. Sex outside marriage. In short, the degeneration of British life. Not so much a permissive society but a cruel and callous one. I don't like the word permissive. I do not give my permission for these unchristian activities to be taking place. And neither do you.

Suddenly a **Woman** *in the audience screams and the clapping stops.*

Mary Today we have some fantastic guest speakers. Labour peer Lord Longford. The wonderful Bishop Trevor Huddleston. And, of course, a man who needs no introduction, but I'll give him one anyway.

Mouse Woman AAAAGHHHHH! There's a mouse! Mice! There's loads of mice! Aaaahhh! It's running up my leg!!

The **Mouse Woman** *calms down. Elsewhere someone shakes a football rattle and two* **Men** *stand up and start to kiss.*

Onlooker   That's disgusting. Somebody eject them! Homosexual scum! Read this and find out what subversive muck you are!

The **Onlooker** *throws a Bible at them.* **Mary** *ignores all this.*

Mary   Malcolm Muggeridge. Or Marvellous Malcolm as I like to call him. Malcolm recently said – I think this is wonderful, I really do – 'The purpose of the festival is that . . . the relatively few people who are responsible for the moral breakdown of our society will know that they are pitted against.'

Another **Woman** *shrieks, standing up.*

Porn Woman   Someone's pasted pornography into my hymn book! Who would do such a thing?!

Mary   Not just a few reactionary people, but all the people in this country who still love this Light – the Light of the world.'

Porn Woman 2   I've got pornography in my hymn book too! It's disgusting! That shouldn't be humanly possible! Not without a shitload of poppers!

Mary (*continuing*)   I think that deserves a round of applause.

Mary *leads the audience in some restrained applause.*

Porn Woman   Actually I quite like it! Where's the nearest toilet? (*Running out.*) Don't applaud me! Don't applaud me! I'm a God fearing porn lover!

Mary   Then, we shall be hearing from one of our brightest young things. Hit popster, Mr Cliff Richard. Who lives in fear of the advancing finger of Homosexuality et al poking into society on a daily basis. And who can blame him? Oh what's this?

From the balcony a banner is unfurled saying CLIFF FOR QUEEN.

Mary   Ah I see we have some of Cliff's fans in the audience. They like you so much they think you should be royalty Cliff. Cliff for Queen! Well . . . wouldn't that be a dandy idea? Sorry?

Onlooker   Mrs Whitehouse, there are gentlemen in the audience wearing ladies clothing!

*A **Nun** stands up as two other **Nuns** conga down the aisle.*

Nun   That's terrible. It's an abomination. Come to Sister Matic and be saved, come on you bent bastards! Where are you?

Mary   Er . . .

*Some other **Nuns** have started high kicking it down the aisles.*

Mary   May we begin proceedings by singing our opening hymn. How Great Thou Art.

An organ starts to play and a gospel choir sings.

Mary *(sings)*
    O Lord my God! When I in awesome wonder
    Consider all the works Thy hands have made.
    I see the stars, I hear the rolling thunder
    The power throughout the universe displayed.
    Then sings my soul, my Saviour God to thee
    How great Thou art. How great Thou art
    Then sings my soul, my Saviour God to thee
    How great thou art, how great thou art!

*During this the pandemonium in the auditorium increases with frenetecism as **Security Guards** rush in and manhandle the **Nuns** out, battering them as they go. More **Women** are carted out brusquely.*

Toilet Woman   I'm just an innocent housewife going to the toilet!

*The **Security Guard** lets her go.*

Toilet Woman   Fuck for Jesus!

He grabs her again and drags her out as some members of the Klu Klux Klan enter.

KKK Leader   We have come to burn all perverts at the stake.

Billy *runs down the aisle dressed as a Priest. He waves a cucumber in the air.*

Billy   Oral sex gives you vitamins! Oral sex gives you vitamins!

Mary *recognises him.*

Mary   William!

Billy   Lick a lezzy today Mary! You should try it!

Mary   William, what have you done?!

Mary *storms off the stage.* **Billy** *jumps on it and grabs the microphone. He takes a booklet out and starts to read.*

Billy   We are representatives of the Gay Liberation Front and this is our manifesto. We believe that all people atracted to their own sex should be brought up to believe that it's normal.

A **Policeman** *runs on and grabs* **Billy***, trying to rescue the microphone off him.* **Billy** *resists.*

Policeman   Come on pervert!

Billy   We believe that psychiatrists should stop treating homosexuality as an illness. We believe that . . .

The **Policeman** *drags him off.* **Billy** *drops the microphone but keeps on shouting.*

Billy   Gay is good! Gay is good!

Blackout.

Scene Two – Hospital, 1986

Mickey *lies in bed. Eventually* **Tom** *enters with a beaker of water and hands it to him.*

Tom   Your Mother's gone home. I could lie. Say she's got a busy week. Say Melanie needs her. Melanie does need her. But what's the point?

Mickey   What's Melanie like?

Tom   Ellie cossets her.

Mickey   I'm gonna die without meeting her.

Tom   Ellie's worried what the neighbours'll think. I don't care any more.

Pause.

Tom   Sorry. I'm unsure of the etiquette.

Mickey   Don't ask how I am. It's impolite. Don't ask how I'm feeling either.

Tom   Impolite too?

Mickey   None of your business.

Tom   Okay.

Mickey   I'm sick of thinking about how I'm feeling. Explaining how I'm feeling.

Tom   Okay.

Mickey   But don't you dare sit there and not ask me how I'm feeling. Coz that drives me nuts. You can't brush me under the carpet.

Tom   So basically. I can't win.

Mickey   Basically who d'you have to fuck to get some pain relief round here?

Tom   Where does it hurt?

Mickey   Where doesn't it?

Tom I'm so sorry Michael.

And he buries his head in the bed and sobs his heart out in silence.
Mickey *just sees the jerky fall and rise of his shoulders.*

Mickey Not brilliantly helpful.

Tom Sorry.

Mickey Do you have any regrets Dad?

Tom Of course!! Of course I do! Look at you!

Mickey I regret I fucked a violinist in 1981. And I've never been to Leningrad.

Tom *smiles.*

Mickey I want you to say I died of AIDS. I don't want euphemisms. I'm disappearing into silence and I don't like it. I want to be screaming, even when I'm tulips. I know you never got me.

Tom I get you. I get you more than you know.

Mickey I never set out to hurt you.

Tom Nor have you.

Mickey But I dreamt. I dreamt that one day I'd walk down a street with my lover and we'd hold hands and no-one'd snigger. I'd switch on the TV and see grown men kissing. Adverts for condoms in the breaks. I dreamt that one day a kid could come out at school and that'd be okay. That dream kept me fighting.

Tom I have one big regret. That I never told you.

Mickey What?

Tom *hesitates. Eventually.*

Tom How proud I was of you. Able to be yourself and stuff the consequences. You may be dying Michael. But there's more life in you than there's ever been in me.

Mickey I never found love. I never went looking. I was gonna change the world first. Do all that later.

Tom   Better than finding it and turning it away.

Mickey   I'm scared Dad.

Tom   I know you are Michael.

Mickey   Alone. You're always on your own.

Tom   I'm not going anywhere Michael. I'll set up camp in the corridor if I have to. I'm not leaving your side.

Mickey   But work . . .

Tom   Can wait.

Mickey   It's not like you.

Mickey *takes his father's hand. Just then* **Russell** *comes in with two coffees. Neither of them are aware of him coming in.*

Mickey   The night I told you I was gay. You threw up. I heard you. In the back garden. By the dahlias.

Tom   I wasn't repulsed by you. How could I be?

Mickey   You got in the car. And went driving. But you took off so fast. Like you wanted to drive yourself off a cliff.

Tom   It was a shock. I was so wrapped up in me and my problems. I never even considered that you might be too.

Mickey   What problems?

Tom   I never hated you Michael. I envied you.

Mickey *doesn't understand.*

Mickey   I might be what too?

Tom   Mickey. I'm . . .

But just then **Mickey** *screams out in agony.* **Russell** *is frozen.*

Tom   I'll call a nurse. I'm so sorry. I'll call a . . .

He sees **Russell** *standing there.*

Tom   Well don't just stand there. Get someone!

The **Nurse** *comes in.*

Nurse   Okay Mickey. We'll give you some more morphine.

She attends to **Mickey**.

Russell   You might be what? Tom?

Tom   Sweet Jesus, what have I done?

Russell *comes and holds* **Mickey***'s hand.* **Tom** *gets up and looks out of the window.*

Blackout.

Scene Three – Police Station, 1971

Billy *sits in his cassock in a dark, damp police cell, turning a navy blue handkerchief over and over in his hands, nervously. Suddenly the door opens and* **Tom** *comes in.* **Billy** *is gobsmacked to see him.* **Billy** *seems a bit manic, unable to settle, almost on the verge of hysteria at times.*

Tom   So. Arrested for playing silly beggars up Westminster Hall.

Billy   Well I suppose you would see it that way, fascist. Or if I may be so bold. Self loathing fascist.

Tom   It's been . . . how long? Ellie and I moved down when she was . . .

Billy   I'm part of a movement.

Tom   You're an activist?

Billy   I'm strong now. I've got clarity. Gay is good. Say it often enough and it becomes true. Try.

Tom   You're all right.

Billy *gets up and paces the room.*

Billy   You know it's liberating, being in a room full of gay people. They even organise dances. Rooms full of gay people dancing. Can you imagine that?

Tom   I'm not sure I'd want to.

Billy   We're Britain's youngest civil rights movement. We might even start a magazine. We did our first demo on Highbury Fields. Your lot nicked a guy caught cottaging there so a hundred and fifty of us went down there with candles and . . . it was so special.

Tom   So. You've started a revolution.

Billy   I dunno if it's a revolution or a party.

Tom   Tune in, turn on, drop out?

Billy   You should come to a meeting Tom. Or come on our next zap. There's this book. Everything You Wanted To Know About Sex But Were Too Afraid To Ask by David Reuben. Or to give him his full medical title, David Reuben. It's full of dangerous misleading inaccuracies. It says gay men shove light bulbs up their arses for sexual gratification. A load of us have been collecting, well, nicking, lightbulbs for ages. We're going to go to Pan Books. The publishers. And scatter like . . . hundreds and hundreds of lightbulbs over the floor of their reception. You see? No-one's gonna get hurt. And it might make people think.

Tom   I'm busy that day.

Billy   Staying in and washing your truncheon?

Tom *smiles.*

Billy   Today was a scream. I loved every minute of it.

Tom   You've been arrested for using a cucumber obscenely. All sounds a bit childish to me.

Billy   These people. These idiots who call themselves Christians. They're so concerned about what I get up to in bed, yet they have complete disinterest in the starvation and murder of people in Bangladesh. Is my sex life really more vital than that?

Tom   Sounds like it is to you.

Billy   It's not all about sex Tom. As you well know. Women and gay people are the litmus test of whether a society respects human rights. We're the canaries in the mine.

Tom   Try and calm down Billy. You seem a bit manic. A bit . . . obsessed.

Billy   Can you blame me?

Tom   I have to get back to my duties. It's good to see you Billy.

Billy   I hope one day you find some peace.

Tom   Ditto.

And he heads to the door.

Billy   Tom?

Tom *looks back.*

Billy   I forgive you. I just want you to know.

Tom   In a way it'd be easier to deal with if you hated me.

Billy   How's Ellie?

Tom   Fine.

Billy   Kids?

Tom   A boy. He's a handful. We'd like another.

Billy   I bet you're a lovely Dad.

At the door **Tom** *hovers.*

Tom   It would be a travesty. If I were to leave the door unlocked accidentally and you miraculously escaped. Wouldn't it?

Billy *nods.* **Tom** *stands aside.*

Tom   Quick.

Billy *gets up and goes to the door.*

Billy   Tom . . .

Tom Quick.

Billy *grabs him and hugs him. Then runs out.* **Tom** *goes and sits on the bench where* **Tom** *was sitting. He has left the hankie behind. He sits looking at it. Then puts it in his pocket. After a while he stands. He walks to the door and looks out.*

Tom Sarge? Sarge! Someone's left the door open. Suspect's done a runner! Sarge!!

He heads out. The lights fade.

Scene Four – Hospital, 1986

Mickey *lies, very sick, wearing an oxygen mask. Around his bed sit* **Russell**, **Tom** *and the* **Nurse**. *As* **Russell** *speaks, so* **Mickey** *gets more and more agitated. By the time* **Russell** *finishes* **Mickey** *is trying to take his oxygen mask off.* **Russell**, **Tom** *and the* **Nurse** *are wearing regulation yellow plastic aprons.* **Mickey** *is wrapped in a red Russian flag.*

Russell Mickey? I'm going to speak to you now. And then after I've spoken we're gonna take your mask off and you can tell us what you think. Okay? Mickey, you've not got very long left. And what the doctors wanted us to ask you was. Do you want us to stop the drugs that are treating you and just keep going with the drugs that stop everything hurting? Or do you want us to keep going with the drugs that are treating you too? They're not doing much good at the moment but we can keep on with them if that's what you want. Mickey, the Nurse is going to take this off now so you can speak. It's okay Mickey. Just . . . have a think and tell us what you want to do.

The **Nurse** *takes the mask off.*

Nurse Here we go.

Mickey *(indicating the flag)*   What is this?

Mickey *puts the mask back on.*

Tom   Your friend the miner sent it. And his wife. They heard you were ill and . . . the red flag?

Mickey *thinks and then nods. He taps the mask. The* **Nurse** *removes it.*

Mickey   I have something very important to tell you.

They all wait with baited breath.

Mickey   I am not the son of Eva Peron.

He gasps for air. The **Nurse** *replaces the mask. His eyes shut.* **Tom**, **Russell** *and the* **Nurse** *freeze, unsure if he has died.*

Russell   I don't want his last words to be gibberish.

Tom   I think we'll carry on with the treatment.

Nurse   It's too late.

Russell *stands.*

Russell   I promise. I'll change. I'll be out, proud. I'll do it. Don't go yet.

Tom   Russell, don't upset yourself.

Russell   I'll make you proud Mickey. Fuck 'em. I'll change the system, not me. You watch Mickey. You watch. I'll be the most famous gay actor in the world!

Tom *stands and hugs* **Russell**. *They cling onto each other for support as* **Russell** *cries.*

An orchestral version of 'Don't Cry For Me Argentina' plays and **Ellie** *comes in in her fur coat and watches. She approaches the bed and pokes* **Mickey**. *She removes the mask.*

Ellie   Your Father's gay.

Mickey   I'm dead. You can't have everything.

Ellie   What's it like?

Mickey   Slow.

Ellie   Like Handel. I had to prop my eyes open with matchsticks every time I played him.

Mickey Dad's . . . really?

Ellie *nods.*

Mickey But he was always such a bad dresser.

Ellie Mr Crimplene. I know.

Mickey Why did you turn your back on me?

Ellie Guilt. I felt we'd made you that way. That he'd made you that way. And by confronting you I'd've had to confront him. And then when you were ill. It was like we'd made you that way too. And instead of apologising. I ran away. I'm good at that. I have lots of practice. Was I awful?

Mickey Yes. But you weren't unusual.

Ellie I'm very normal. It's one of the things I hate about me.

Mickey You're not normal. You can play the organ.

Ellie Not any more. Doesn't make me happy the way it used to.

Mickey Why are you here?

Ellie To make it up to you.

Mickey How?

Ellie How d'you think?

Mickey Eh?

Ellie Shh!

Mickey What?

Ellie Hold on tight.

Mickey Why?

She sits up on the bed, keeping her legs up off the floor.

Ellie I don't want you falling out.

She lifts up the bar at the side of the bed.

Ellie   Where d'you want to go? You can go anywhere in the world. Where shall we go?

Mickey   I'd love to see the Winter Palace. Can you do that? Leningrad?

Ellie (*nods*)   They call it St Petersburg now.

Mickey   Why?

Ellie   I'll tell you on the way.

The stage darkens and the bed hovers in mid air. Wind blows and the bed moves. The music grows louder. **Ellie** *and* **Mickey** *are on a magic carpet ride, bobbing up and down.* **Mickey** *becomes agitated.*

Mickey   No.

Ellie   What?

Mickey   This isn't right.

Ellie   It's what you always wanted. The carpet, in church.

Mickey   I know you can't go on magic carpet rides.

Ellie   You can!

Mickey   I was just trying to get your attention!

Ellie   But we're going now.

Mickey   I don't want you with me. Ever.

Ellie   I can't hear you. We're up in the clouds.

Mickey   You never could Mum. Even when I was screaming.

And they fly off. The music soars.

Blackout.

Scene Five – Hotel room, 2009

Russell *in a hotel room, dabbing coke round his gums as he speaks on his Iphone.*

Russell   Your Name In Lights is going to be fabulous. I'd bet my life on it. It's going to put musical theatre centre stage on prime time television and make the public into stars. I'm so excited. You must come to one of the recordings James. It's gonna be so camp, I can't wait. And some of the girls they've found are so fucking talented. I'm really looking forward to working with them. All of them. It's my dream job. I think the ratings are gonna go through the roof. It's what Saturday night's crying out for. Good old fashioned entertainment that means something, you know? Yeah you too, oh it's so good talking to you again James. Yeah you too and thanks for all your support, means a lot. Yeah you too James. Don't go changing!

He hangs up just as **Toby**, *a younger guy, walks in. He is dressed in a top and his undies. He looks very like Mickey. It shocks* **Russell**.

Russell   Mickey.

Toby   God, can't you even remember my name? You really know how to make a girl feel special.

Russell   For a second there I thought you were . . . you really remind me of . . . Oh it was years ago.

Russell *chops up some lines on a mirror on the bed.* **Toby** *lies back.*

Toby   Have you got to speak to any more journalists?

Russell   No.

Toby   Well go on then.

Russell   What?

Toby   Fuck me.

Russell   Now where did I put my jonnnies?

Toby   Jonnies? You call them jonnies?

Russell   I'm an old man. Have you got any?

Toby   Babe. As it said on my profile. I'm into BB.

Russell   I thought that stood for Big Brother.

Toby   Bareback rider, baby! All saddled up. C'mon cowboy.
(*Brokeback Mountain*) I don't know how to quit you Ennis.

Russell   Prick.

Toby   I like the sensation. Skin on skin. Can't beat it.

Russell   Toby . . .

Toby   I know you want me. You brought me back to your
hotel for a drink. A drink. I've seen the way you look at me.
I wear a tight tee shirt to rehearsals. For your benefit. I see
you looking at my tits. You like my tits, don't you Russell?

Russell   Do I?

Russell *snorts a line.*

Toby   You like my arse as well. Just here. It's yours babe.

Russell   What if I'm HIV?

Toby   We'll never know will we?

Russell   Oh but you might.

Toby   I wanna catch your bugs baby.

Russell *is stunned.*

Toby   OMG. Are you?

Russell   Shouldn't you treat everyone like they are?

Toby   Loser!

Russell   Why am I a loser?

Toby   If you are and stuff.

Russell   I'll ask again.

Toby It's easy enough to avoid.

Russell And some of us popped our cherries before the word was even invented darling! You know, I look at you . . .

Toby So what if you do give me something. I'll just take pills. Fuck it.

Russell . . . and you remind me of someone.

Toby Jake Gyllenhaal, don't tell me Russ.

Russell Only he was generous where you're selfish.

Toby I'm giving you my arse? And I'm selfish?

Russell He believed in something.

Toby I believe you're mixing me up with someone who gives a shit, Russell.

Russell What do you really believe in Toby?

Toby I'm just looking after number one baby.

Russell He had a brain. 'Til the cytomeglavirus ate away at it.

Toby HIV's like an old man's disease. It's so last century.

Russell *suddenly lashes out, knocking* **Toby**'*s face, so he falls backward on the bed. He stands over him.* **Toby** *now looks shocked.*

Russell Me and my mates went through shit to let you be this apathetic! Fighting our corner so that queens like you wouldn't be scared! Have some fucking respect for your elders!

Toby Elders? What is this, a cult?

Russell No dear. The only cult round here is you. (*Tuts.*) Your elders, your ancestors, the queens who went before you! Don't piss on their graves!

Toby So you are then.

Russell Honest answer? I don't know.

Toby   Have a test.

Russell   I had a test before you were probably even born darling.

Toby (*Clutching his jaw.*)   Bastard.

Russell   You wanna talk dirty darling, go right ahead. Want it rough? You can have it rough. If that's what makes you like me then fine. If that's what gay community means these days hoorah. Let's do it. But don't take the piss or you'll get another slap.

Russell *is almost embarrassed by his outburst. He backs off*.

Toby   I'm not . . . totally cool with this scene.

Russell   Where's your attitude now Toby? Said online you had rape fantasies.

Toby   You're like seriously weird Russell.

Russell   I'm so glad the future of our community is in your hands.

Toby   West End Wendy? TV's Mr Nice Guy? Queer Next Door? Psycho AIDS twat!

Russell   I was! But three weeks ago my health adviser tells me that thanks to another kind of drug there's no detectable virus in my body!

Toby   Well that's good isn't it?

Russell   And then two weeks ago my lover of two years walks out on me because. Because he was prepared to live with me when he thought I might be dying, but not when I might actually live.

Toby   Says a lot about your personality.

Russell   So forgive me if I'm a little bit all over the place.

Russell *sits down. He buries his head in his hands*.

Russell   That's why I'm in a hotel. Go home Toby.

Toby   Start again? Pretend this never happened?

Russell   I want to do something right. Just once.

Toby   Do me.

Russell   I hit you Toby. Have some self respect.

Toby *looks at him, and then slowly walks out of the door.* **Russell** *takes another line of coke. He sits there thinking, then picks up the phone. He punches in a number. Then steels himself.*

Russell   Just once.

He takes a deep breath then punches in the final number.

Russell   Hi James? It's Russell Dowler again, sorry to call you back. Look I know you're just the showbiz reporter but . . . I've got this scoop and I just want it to get out there. You know that Chief of Police guy? Tom Harris? (*Beat.*) Whenever he talks about his family he talks about his son dying in a motorbike accident. Well he didn't. He had AIDS. He was one of the first people in this country to die from it. (*Beat.*) He's a liar. Do we really want someone like that in charge of law and order? (*Beat.*) Oh and another thing. Tom Harris is as gay as you and me. Dig for dirt mate. You'll find it. It's your job. I really appreciate your support James. Don't go changing! (*He hangs up. Raises a glass to the sky, very Norma Desmond.*) I used to be huge, but I just got bigger!

Blackout.

Scene Six – A roundabout in Tring, 2010

As earlier the body of the **Boy** *on the ground.* **Ellie** *floats in, flying down on a parachute.*

Ellie   Nearly home.

She lands. The parachute covers the stage. She looks to the **Boy***.*

Ellie   I'm sorry but I don't think you're my son. He's up there. Floating around looking for St Petersburg. I wanted to go with him but he kicked me off. Fortunately I'd packed this.

She goes about gathering up the parachute.

Ellie   I tried to make amends. I tried to seek his forgiveness. I didn't get it. But that's okay. I realise now that's just something that I'll have to live with. I'm an unforgiven mother. And that's fine. It's all I deserve. There's nothing I can do to change that. I let him down. All I can try and do now is . . . try not to let myself down.

She realises the **Boy** *is whimpering.*

Ellie   Are you all right?

He sits up. He is still covered in blood.

Boy   I was walking through town. So many lights, I thought I was safe. They fell in alongside me. Can only have been about fifteen. Sixteen tops. Start pushing me. 'You a batty boy?' They'd followed me from the pub. I was gonna leave with my mates but they were getting a cab and I'm skint. I tried to leg it but they tripped me up and that's when I heard breaking glass and saw the bottle. 'Shove it up his arse. Batty boy like that'. Talking black but they're white. Two girls with them. Filming it on their phones. I'm probably on Youtube by now. (*Beat.*) Will you help me?

Ellie *gulps.*

Ellie   Of course.

Boy   I can't remember who I am.

Ellie   It's okay.

She starts to wrap him up in the parachute to stem the blood.

Ellie   Please. Just try not to move.

Boy   I can't remember.

Ellie   What do you remember?

Boy   Their laughter.

Ellie   Don't close your eyes.

Boy   What are you going to do?

Ellie (*calls*)   Can somebody help me please?!! PLEASE CAN SOMEONE HELP!!!

Boy   You're a kind person.

Ellie   You were meeting someone. A date. Eight o'clock outside the station. This is a new shirt.

Boy   You're lovely.

Ellie   We'll clean it up. And get you to the station. Bright as a new pin.

She kneels and cradles him in her arms as he dies. She screams at the top of her voice.

Ellie   PLEASE!! SOMEONE!! HELP ME!!!!!

As she screams thunder roars and lightning flashes across the sky.

Blackout.

Scene Seven – Billy's house, 2000

A dark night. A thunderstorm. **Billy** *returns home from a club with a guy he has picked up,* **Tony**. **Tony** *is a bit pissed. They are both in their late 50s.*

Billy   I think someone's had a bit too much to drink.

Tony   What's your name again?

Billy   Billy. Take a seat. Can I get you some more?

Tony   Lager?

Billy   Lager it is then. Think I'll join you.

Billy *gets two cans of lager out of his pockets.* **Tony** *falls back into a hard backed chair.*

Billy   Da-nah! Nicked 'em from the club.

He hands him one.

Billy My drink of choice used to be Guinness. But your tastes change don't they?

Tony Yeah.

Billy We were the oldest queens in that place tonight weren't we? By about seventy years.

Tony Did we kiss in the cab?

Billy We did mate, yeah.

Billy *runs his hand over* **Tony**'s *chest. His fingers linger over* **Tony**'s *nipple.* **Tony** *laughs.* **Billy** *squeezes it. Hard.* **Tony** *responds.*

Billy Like that do you? Thought you might. (*Squeezes again.*)

Billy *takes his scarf off.*

Tony I am splattered.

Billy Shall we tie you up? Hey? Lock you up and throw away the key?

Billy *ties* **Tony** *to the chair with his scarf.*

Billy What's your name?

Tony Tony.

Billy Tony. Well if it's all right, Tony, I'll call you by your proper name. Doctor McKinnon.

Tony *flinches.*

Billy Sorry about the mess. I wasn't expecting company so . . .

Tony Who are you?

Billy You see I recognised you as soon as I walked into that place. I saw you and I physically recoiled. And then I went to the toilets and I threw up.

Tony   I don't know what you're talking about.

Billy   But then me and vomit. That's something you're used to.

Tony *makes a small whimper like an animal in distress.*

Billy   I've dreamt about meeting you. You are my recurring dream. And here you are. Forty years on. Live in my own front room. And I find you in a fucking gay club.

I wondered maybe whether I was wrong.

Tony   You are.

Billy   When hallelujah you offer me a line. We go to the toilets, where only moments earlier I have vomited at the sight of you. And you get out your wallet. And you chop us up some lines. With your credit card. Which you then give me to lick. So of course. Like any Jessica Fletcher in the making, I check your name. Doctor McKinnon.

(*Pause.*)

Why did you do it?

Tony   It was a lifetime away.

Billy   Do you remember me or do we all blur into one?

Tony   What's your name?

Billy   Billy Lynch. You called me William. You gave me Guinness. I lay for three days in a bed filled with my own shit, piss and vomit. While you showed me those pictures. Pictures of naked men. And you played those tapes. Calling me a dirty queer. It was your voice, Doctor McKinnon. I could hear the other patients. Crying. Screaming. All night. You made me wank over pictures of Tom and you watched and injected me and then you brought out the electrodes.

He takes a deep breath. He continues.

Billy   You. Live up here (*indicates his head*) practically every night. And I don't even register with you!

Tony   It was my job.

Billy   I was only obeying orders?!

Tony   We were told you'd all asked to be there.

Billy   I chose it over a prison sentence.

Tony   You chose.

Billy   Don't argue with me. You're not in a position to argue!

(*Pause.*)

Did you hate yourself that much? Or is it that that made you gay? Seeing all those images. Not got much to say for yourself have you?

Tony   Look, untie me. Then I'll say sorry. And then it'll mean something.

Billy   Shut up!

Billy *kneels and cries.*

Tony   I hated myself. What I did to you I did to me. And for that I am sorry. I remember you now. I do.

Billy   Don't lie!

Tony   You were one of the pretty ones. It was. A very long time ago. You have nightmares? This. This is my nightmare.

Pause. **Billy** *gets up and we see he is holding a bread knife.*

Tony   Please . . . I've changed.

Billy   You're still there. You'll always be there.

Tony   Even if you hurt me I may still be there.

Billy   Since I met you. I've fought. That people like me wouldn't feel what you made me feel. Gay is good. Gay is . . .

Tony   Please.

Billy   But on my own. With men. I feel. Scared.

Tony   People like us.

Billy   I need to get to the bottom of what your sickness is.

Tony   No.

Billy *is approaching him now.*

Billy   It won't hurt. Tony. Anthony. It'll be . . . just like . . . a trip to the dentist.

Tony *whimpers as* **Billy** *steps forward and plunges the breadknife into his chest.* **Tony** *eyes widen in terror. Then he slumps forward in his chair.* **Billy** *rearranges him neatly on the chair, the breadknife jutting out of his chest.* **Billy** *takes a swig from his can of lager.*

Blackout.

Scene Eight – Tom's house, Islington, 2010/Tom's back garden, Islington, 2010/Tom's old front garden, Billericay, 1999

Tom *stands thinking, running the blue hankie over and over in his hands.* **Melanie** *comes in.*

Melanie   My therapist's going to have a field day. (*Beat.*) I just phoned home. Arabella's hyper. I said 'Guess what sweetheart? You have a gay granddad.' And then I burst out crying. How are you feeling?

Tom   Dangerous question. I've cut myself off from feelings over the years.

Melanie   Why didn't you tell me the truth?

Tom   About Michael? We thought it'd be for the best.

Melanie   About you.

Russell *enters.*

Tom   I couldn't even be honest with myself.

Melanie   You don't do things by halves do you? Most people sit their families down and come out to them quietly. You assemble the world's Press.

Tom   I've been such a coward.

Melanie   What are you going to say to them?

Russell   The six million dollar question.

Tom looks at him.

Russell   I know that look. It's Glinda to Dorothy when she lands in Oz. 'Are you a good witch or a bad witch?'

Melanie   Do you have to be such a stereotype?

Russell   Oh, so you're more impressed by the queens who get married and have kids and hide their love away?

Tom   Go easy on him, Melanie. He might well be a good witch.

Russell   I'm sorry if I'm a stereotype, I'm just being me. And . . . (*this is a struggle*) I'm sorry that Mickey went and I stayed.

Melanie   What a ridiculous thing to say.

*Russell thinks. **Ellie** comes in carrying **Mickey**'s guitar.*

Ellie   Look what I found in the loft.

Tom   Where've you been?

She sits, tuning it.

Ellie   Tring? Mount Ararat? The swirling mists of time were particularly pleasant. And very nearly St Petersburg.

Melanie   Are you going to apologise to me?

Ellie   Of course. I am very sorry about your Care Bears Nightie going missing that time. I actually attacked it with some crinkle cut scissors because you were really getting on my tits that day. I'm sorry. Same when your Girls World was mysteriously shaved. Mea culpa.

Melanie   I had a brother who was amazing and inspirational and you made me think he was just a shit motorcyclist!

Ellie   Oh that.

Russell   Yes that.

Tom   Are you leaving me?

Ellie   This house is one of the few things in life that gives me pleasure. Whether I share it with you or not is immaterial.

Melanie   Are you all right Mother?

Ellie   Yes Melanie. I've got my mojo back. That's what happens when you hover two hundred metres above the earth on a magic carpet. You see the truth. (*To* **Tom**.) You know, it's funny . . . your lover being in prison.

Tom   Is it?

Ellie   When I'm just being released.

She picks out a tune on the guitar, quietly and slowly, and starts to hum softly.

Russell   Can I go yet?

Tom   Would you like me to phone you a cab?

Russell   Have the Press gone?

Tom   No, they're still there.

Melanie   But if he steps outside the front door that's practically an admission. You're happy with that?

Russell   I'll be in the back garden. Shout me when it's here.

And he leaves. **Ellie** *starts to sing.*

Ellie   Which side are you on boys?
            Which side are you on?
            Which side are you on boys?
            Which side are you on?

Melanie   What are you saying Dad?

Tom   It's never too late to surprise someone.

Ellie   I'm bound to follow my conscience
And do whatever I can
But it'll take much more than the union law
To knock the fight out of a working man
Which side are you on, boys?
Which side are you on?
Which side are you on, boys?
Which side are you on?

As she sings, **Billy** *comes in and sits on the couch in prison clothes.*

Tom   How is it here?

Billy   The scary thing is. If I had my time all over again. I'd probably still do it. So I guess I'm in the right place. Why are you here?

Tom   I . . .

Billy   Imagine if I'd said you'd attacked me all those years ago. Imagine if they'd believed me. Might be you sat here, eh?

Tom   I understand the blame should be partly mine.

Billy   I wish I'd never met you.

Tom   You were always full of such optimism. About us. The world.

Billy   Not any more.

Tom   I want you to be. I want you to have hope again.

Billy   I can't.

Tom   Forty seven years ago I . . . I was waiting for you when you came out of hospital. I'd . . . I'm prepared to do the same for you now.

Billy   My head's been messed with enough over the years.

Tom   This time I mean it.

Billy   Are you laughing at me?

Tom *shakes his head.*

Tom   You write such lovely letters. I hope mine are okay.

Billy   I wish I'd known your son.

Tom   I wish I'd known him more. (*Sighs.*) I'll give you time to think about this. It might be the worst decision we ever made . . . but

Billy   I might already be spoken for.

Tom   Right.

Billy   I'm not.

Tom   We could grow old together.

Billy   We already are.

Tom   I wish I'd known you. More.

Billy   You didn't do it nearly fifty years ago. And you won't do it now. I'm probably never going to see you again, so . . .

Tom *gets up.*

Tom   One of these days I might surprise you.

They stand and shake hands.

Billy   You won't. You'll never do it, Tom.

Billy *leaves.* **Tom** *takes a piece of paper from his pocket and reads the statement he's prepared to* **Ellie** *and* **Melanie**.

Tom   I know that certain stories have come to light about my relationship with William Lynch and the death of my son from AIDS in 1986. Because of my catalogue of lies for the past half a century my family is now suffering greatly. My son's biggest fear was disappearing into silence. He wanted to be screaming. Even when he was tulips. And so I must not go coyly, head bowed. I do not regret who I am, but I do regret my deceptive behaviour over the years. And it is because of this deception that I forthwith offer my resignation to the police force. I have misled the public too long. I have misled those I love longer. It's time to be honest. Because tomorrow, we're tulips.

Ellie *wipes a tear from her eye.*

Melanie   Do you want me to come and hold your hand?

Tom   I have to do this alone.

Melanie *nods.* **Russell** *comes into the back garden. He looks up to the stars. In the living room.* **Tom** *looks to* **Ellie**.

Tom   Wish me luck?

Ellie   Go. If you're going.

Tom   Look after your Mother.

Melanie *nods. He turns and faces the door.*

Russell   Mickey? Can you hear me?

The lights come up on another part of the stage and their old front garden in Billericay. **Tom**, **Melanie** *and* **Ellie** *turn to see sixteen year old* **Mickey** *running into their front garden in his Mum's wedding dress. Sixteen year old* **Russell** *runs after him dressed in a multicoloured frock.* **Russell** *watches them from his garden.*

Mickey   Come on Russell! You're my bridesmaid!

Russell   What's my name?

Mickey   Dolores May!

Russell   No it's not it's Barbara Jean! You're Dolores May!

Mickey   Shut up and spin.

They both stand there spinning.

Russell   Why are we doing this?

Mickey   To try and catch up with the world. The world spins.

Russell   I know that.

Mickey   Spin, Russell!!

Russell   It makes you dizzy!

Mickey   One day. One day I'm gonna spin so fast . . . I'm gonna fly off the world!

They continue to spin. **Tom** *breaks away and heads to the front door.* **Ellie** *and* **Melanie** *stand watching the boys spinning.* **Russell** *watches too.*

Ellie   Michael? Are you wearing my wedding dress again?!

Mickey   No!

This tickles **Russell**.

Ellie   Wait 'til your Father gets home!

The boys continue to spin. **Tom** *opens the front door and a hundred camera lights flash, sending beams of light across the stage.*

Blackout.

Methuen Drama Student Editions

Jean Anouilh *Antigone* • John Arden *Serjeant Musgrave's Dance*
Alan Ayckbourn *Confusions* • Aphra Behn *The Rover* • Edward Bond
Lear • *Saved* • Bertolt Brecht *The Caucasian Chalk Circle* • *Fear and
Misery in the Third Reich* • *The Good Person of Szechwan* • *Life of Galileo* •
Mother Courage and her Children• *The Resistible Rise of Arturo Ui* • *The
Threepenny Opera* • Anton Chekhov *The Cherry Orchard* • *The Seagull* •
Three Sisters • *Uncle Vanya* • Caryl Churchill *Serious Money* • *Top Girls*
• Shelagh Delaney *A Taste of Honey* • Euripides *Elektra* • *Medea*•
Dario Fo *Accidental Death of an Anarchist* • Michael Frayn *Copenhagen*
• John Galsworthy *Strife* • Nikolai Gogol *The Government Inspector* •
Robert Holman *Across Oka* • Henrik Ibsen *A Doll's House* • *Ghosts*•
Hedda Gabler • Charlotte Keatley *My Mother Said I Never Should* •
Bernard Kops *Dreams of Anne Frank* • Federico García Lorca *Blood
Wedding* • *Doña Rosita the Spinster* (bilingual edition) •*The House of
Bernarda Alba* • (bilingual edition) • *Yerma* (bilingual edition) • David
Mamet *Glengarry Glen Ross* • *Oleanna* • Patrick Marber *Closer* • John
Marston *Malcontent* • Martin McDonagh *The Lieutenant of Inishmore* •
Joe Orton *Loot* • Luigi Pirandello *Six Characters in Search of an Author*
• Mark Ravenhill *Shopping and F***ing* • Willy Russell *Blood Brothers*
• *Educating Rita* • Sophocles *Antigone* • *Oedipus the King* • Wole
Soyinka *Death and the King's Horseman* • Shelagh Stephenson *The
Memory of Water* • August Strindberg *Miss Julie* • J. M. Synge *The
Playboy of the Western World* • Theatre Workshop *Oh What a Lovely
War* Timberlake Wertenbaker *Our Country's Good* • Arnold Wesker
The Merchant • Oscar Wilde *The Importance of Being Earnest* •
Tennessee Williams *A Streetcar Named Desire* • *The Glass Menagerie*

Methuen Drama Modern Classics

Jean Anouilh *Antigone* • Brendan Behan *The Hostage* • Robert Bolt *A Man for All Seasons* • Edward Bond *Saved* • Bertolt Brecht *The Caucasian Chalk Circle* • *Fear and Misery in the Third Reich* • *The Good Person of Szechwan* • *Life of Galileo* • *The Messingkauf Dialogues* • *Mother Courage and Her Children* • *Mr Puntila and His Man Matti* • *The Resistible Rise of Arturo Ui* • *Rise and Fall of the City of Mahagonny* • *The Threepenny Opera* • Jim Cartwright *Road* • *Two & Bed* • Caryl Churchill *Serious Money* • *Top Girls* • Noël Coward *Blithe Spirit* • *Hay Fever* • *Present Laughter* • *Private Lives* • *The Vortex* • Shelagh Delaney *A Taste of Honey* • Dario Fo *Accidental Death of an Anarchist* • Michael Frayn *Copenhagen* • Lorraine Hansberry *A Raisin in the Sun* • Jonathan Harvey *Beautiful Thing* • David Mamet *Glengarry Glen Ross* • *Oleanna* • *Speed-the-Plow* • Patrick Marber *Closer* • *Dealer's Choice* • Arthur Miller *Broken Glass* • Percy Mtwa, Mbongeni Ngema, Barney Simon *Woza Albert!* • Joe Orton *Entertaining Mr Sloane* • *Loot* • *What the Butler Saw* • Mark Ravenhill *Shopping and F***ing* • Willy Russell *Blood Brothers* • *Educating Rita* • *Stags and Hens* • *Our Day Out* • Jean-Paul Sartre *Crime Passionnel* • Wole Soyinka • *Death and the King's Horseman* • Theatre Workshop *Oh, What a Lovely War* • Frank Wedekind • *Spring Awakening* • Timberlake Wertenbaker *Our Country's Good*

Methuen Drama Contemporary Dramatists
include

John Arden (two volumes)
Arden & D'Arcy
Peter Barnes (three volumes)
Sebastian Barry
Dermot Bolger
Edward Bond (eight volumes)
Howard Brenton
  (two volumes)
Richard Cameron
Jim Cartwright
Caryl Churchill (two volumes)
Sarah Daniels (two volumes)
Nick Darke
David Edgar (three volumes)
David Eldridge
Ben Elton
Dario Fo (two volumes)
Michael Frayn (three volumes)
David Greig
John Godber (four volumes)
Paul Godfrey
John Guare
Lee Hall (two volumes)
Peter Handke
Jonathan Harvey
  (two volumes)
Declan Hughes
Terry Johnson (three volumes)
Sarah Kane
Barrie Keeffe
Bernard-Marie Koltès
  (two volumes)
Franz Xaver Kroetz
David Lan
Bryony Lavery
Deborah Levy
Doug Lucie

David Mamet (four volumes)
Martin McDonagh
Duncan McLean
Anthony Minghella
  (two volumes)
Tom Murphy (six volumes)
Phyllis Nagy
Anthony Neilsen (two volumes)
Philip Osment
Gary Owen
Louise Page
Stewart Parker (two volumes)
Joe Penhall (two volumes)
Stephen Poliakoff
  (three volumes)
David Rabe (two volumes)
Mark Ravenhill (two volumes)
Christina Reid
Philip Ridley
Willy Russell
Eric-Emmanuel Schmitt
Ntozake Shange
Sam Shepard (two volumes)
Wole Soyinka (two volumes)
Simon Stephens (two volumes)
Shelagh Stephenson
David Storey (three volumes)
Sue Townsend
Judy Upton
Michel Vinaver
  (two volumes)
Arnold Wesker (two volumes)
Michael Wilcox
Roy Williams (three volumes)
Snoo Wilson (two volumes)
David Wood (two volumes)
Victoria Wood

Methuen Drama World Classics

include

Jean Anouilh (two volumes)
Brendan Behan
Aphra Behn
Bertolt Brecht (eight volumes)
Büchner
Bulgakov
Calderón
Čapek
Anton Chekhov
Noël Coward (eight volumes)
Feydeau (two volumes)
Eduardo De Filippo
Max Frisch
John Galsworthy
Gogol
Gorky (two volumes)
Harley Granville Barker
    (two volumes)
Victor Hugo
Henrik Ibsen (six volumes)
Jarry

Lorca (three volumes)
Marivaux
Mustapha Matura
David Mercer (two volumes)
Arthur Miller (six volumes)
Molière
Musset
Peter Nichols (two volumes)
Joe Orton
A. W. Pinero
Luigi Pirandello
Terence Rattigan
    (two volumes)
W. Somerset Maugham
    (two volumes)
August Strindberg
    (three volumes)
J. M. Synge
Ramón del Valle-Inclán
Frank Wedekind
Oscar Wilde

Methuen Drama Classical Greek Dramatists

Aeschylus Plays: One
(Persians, Seven Against Thebes, Suppliants,
Prometheus Bound)

Aeschylus Plays: Two
(Oresteia: Agamemnon, Libation-Bearers, Eumenides)

Aristophanes Plays: One
(Acharnians, Knights, Peace, Lysistrata)

Aristophanes Plays: Two
(Wasps, Clouds, Birds, Festival Time, Frogs)

Aristophanes & Menander: New Comedy
(Women in Power, Wealth, The Malcontent,
The Woman from Samos)

Euripides Plays: One
(Medea, The Phoenician Women, Bacchae)

Euripides Plays: Two
(Hecuba, The Women of Troy, Iphigeneia at Aulis,
Cyclops)

Euripides Plays: Three
(Alkestis, Helen, Ion)

Euripides Plays: Four
(Elektra, Orestes, Iphigeneia in Tauris)

Euripides Plays: Five
(Andromache, Herakles' Children, Herakles)

Euripides Plays: Six
(Hippolytos, Suppliants, Rhesos)

Sophocles Plays: One
(Oedipus the King, Oedipus at Colonus, Antigone)

Sophocles Plays: Two
(Ajax, Women of Trachis, Electra, Philoctetes)